펼쳐 보면 느껴집니다

단 한 줄도 배움의 공백이 생기지 않도록
문장 한 줄마다 20년이 넘는
해커스의 영어교육 노하우를 담았음을

덮고 나면 확신합니다

수많은 선생님의 목소리와
정확한 출제 데이터 분석으로 꽉 찬
교재 한 권이면 충분함을

해커스북 중·고등
HackersBook.com

WHY
HACKERS
GRAMMAR SMART?

Completely master English grammar

누구나 쉽게
이해할 수 있는

간결한 문법 설명

실생활에서 그대로
사용할 수 있는

유용한 표현과 예문

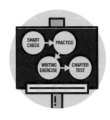

Smart Check → Practice →
Writing Exercise →
Chapter Test로 이어지는

단계별 문제 풀이

HACKERS
Grammar Smart

Starter

HACKERS
Grammar Smart

Level 1

HACKERS
Grammar Smart

Level 2

HACKERS
Grammar Smart

Level 3

Effectively prepare for middle school English exams

학교 시험 기출경향을
완벽 반영한 문제로

서술형 포함 내신 완벽 대비

풍부한 문제의 Workbook과
다양한 부가 학습 자료로

학습효과 Up Up!

Hackers Grammar Smart 시리즈를 검토해주신 선생님들

경기

강무정	광교EIE고려대학교어학원
강민정	김진성의 열정어학원
김민성	빨리강해지는학원
윤혜영	이루다영어수학학원
이창석	정현영어학원
이창헌	더블원영어학원
정필두	시흥배곧 정상어학원
조은혜	이든영수학원

최희정	SJ클쌤영어
탁은영	EIE고려대학교어학원 태전퍼스트캠퍼스
한지수	위드유어학원
홍영숙	솔로몬학원
황정민	한수위학원

부산

배미경	삼정아카데미학원
이미영	수영학원

서울

신봉철	강북세일학원
양세희	양세희수능영어학원
이현아	이은재학원
채가희	대성세그루학원
최세아	씨앤씨학원

인천

송인택	변화와도전학원

해커스 어학연구소 자문위원단 3기

강원

박정선	잉글리쉬클럽
최현주	최샘영어

경기

강민정	김진성열정어학원
강상훈	평촌RTS학원
강지인	강지인영어학원
권계미	A&T+ 영어
김미아	김쌤영어학원
김설화	업라이트잉글리쉬
김성재	스윗스터디학원
김세훈	모두의학원
김수아	더스터디(The STUDY)
김영아	백송고등학교
김유경	벨트어학원
김유경	포시즌스어학원
김유동	이스턴어학원
김지숙	위디벨럽학원
김지현	이지프레임영어학원
김해빈	해빛영어학원
김현지	지앤비영어학원
박가영	한민고등학교
박영서	스윗스터디학원
박은별	더킹영수학원
박재홍	록키어학원
성승민	SDH어학원 불당캠퍼스
신소연	Ashley English
오귀연	루나영어학원
유신애	에듀포커스학원
윤소정	ILP이화학원
이동진	이룸학원
이상미	버밍엄영어교습소
이연경	명품M비욘드수학영어학원
이은수	광주세종학원
이지혜	리케이온
이진희	이엠원영수학원
이충기	영어나무
이효명	갈매리드앤톡영어독서학원
임한글	Apsun앞선영어학원
장광명	엠케이영어학원
전상호	평촌이지어학원
전성훈	훈선생영어교실
정선영	코어플러스영어학원
정준	고양외국어고등학교
조연아	카이트학원
채기림	고려대학교EIE영어학원
최지영	다른영어학원
최한나	석사영수전문
최희정	SJ클쌤영어학원
현지환	모두의학원
홍태경	공감국어영어전문학원

경남

강다원	더(the)오르다영어학원
라승희	아이작잉글리쉬
박주언	유니크학원
배송현	두잇영어교습소
안윤서	어썸영어학원
임진희	어썸영어학원

경북

권현민	삼성영어석적우방교실
김으뜸	EIE영어학원 옥계캠퍼스
배세왕	비케이영수전문고등관학원
유영선	아이비티어학원

광주

김유희	김유희영어학원
서희연	SDL영어수학학원
송수일	아이리드영어학원
오진우	SLT어학원수학원
정영철	정영철영어전문학원
최경옥	봉선중학교

대구

권익재	제이슨영어
김명일	독학인학원
김보곤	베스트영어
김연정	달서고등학교
김혜란	김혜란영어학원
문애주	프렌즈입시학원
박정근	공부의힘pnk학원
박희숙	열공열강영어수학학원
신동기	신통외국어학원
위영선	위영선영어학원
윤창원	공터영어학원 상인센터
이승현	학문당입시학원
이주현	이주현영어학원
이헌욱	이헌욱영어학원
장준현	장쌤독해종결영어학원
주현아	민쌤영어학원
최윤정	최강영어학원

대전

곽선영	위드유학원
김지운	더포스둔산학원
박미현	라시움영어대동학원
박세리	EM101학원

부산

김건희	레지나잉글리쉬 영어학원
김미나	위드중고등영어학원
박수진	정모클영어국어학원
박수진	지니잉글리쉬
박인숙	리더스영어전문학원
옥지윤	더цент엄영어학원
윤진희	위니드영어전문교습소
이종혁	진수학원
정혜인	엠티엔영어학원
조정래	알파카의영어농장
주태양	솔라영어학원

서울

Erica Sull	하버드브레인영어학원
강고은	케이앤학원
강신아	교우학원
공현미	이은재어학원
권영진	경동고등학교
김나영	프라임클래스영어학원
김달수	대일외국어고등학교
김대니	채움학원
김문영	창문여자고등학교
김상백	강북세일학원
김정은	강북뉴스터디학원
김혜경	대동세무고등학교
남혜원	함영원입시전문학원
노시은	케이앤학원
박선정	강북세일학원
박수진	이은재어학원
박지수	이플러스영수학원
서승희	함영원입시전문학원
신지웅	강북세일학원
양세희	양세희수능영어학원
우정용	제임스영어앤드학원
이박원	이박원어학원
이승혜	스텔라영어
이정욱	이은재어학원
이지연	중계케이트영어학원
임예찬	학습컨설턴트
장지희	고려대학교사범대학부속고등학교
정미라	미라정영어학원
조민규	조민규영어
채가희	대성세그루영수학원

울산

김기태	그라티아어학원
이민주	로이아카데미
홍영민	더이안영어전문학원

인천

강재민	스터디위드제이쌤
고현순	정상학원
권효진	Genie's English
김솔	전문과외
김정아	밀턴영어학원
서상천	최정서학원
이윤주	트리플원
최예영	영웅아카데미

전남

강희진	강희진영어학원
김두환	해남맨체스터영수학원
송승연	송승연영수학원
윤세광	비상구영어학원

전북

김길자	맨투맨학원
김미영	링크영어학원
김효성	연세입시학원
노빈나	노빈나영어전문학원
라성남	하포드어학원
박재훈	위니드수학지앤비영어학원
박향숙	STA영어전문학원
서종원	서종원영어학원
이상훈	나는학원
장지원	링컨더글라스학원
지근영	한솔영어수학학원
최성령	연세입시학원
최혜영	이든영어수학학원

제주

김랑	KLS어학원
박자은	KLS어학원

충남

김예지	더배움프라임영수학원
김철홍	청경학원
노태겸	최상위학원

충북

라은경	이화윤스영어교습소
신유정	비타민영어클리닉학원

HACKERS
GRAMMAR
SMART STARTER

HACKERS

Contents

Preview

명쾌한 설명과 실용적인 문장으로 Smart하게 학습 ——————

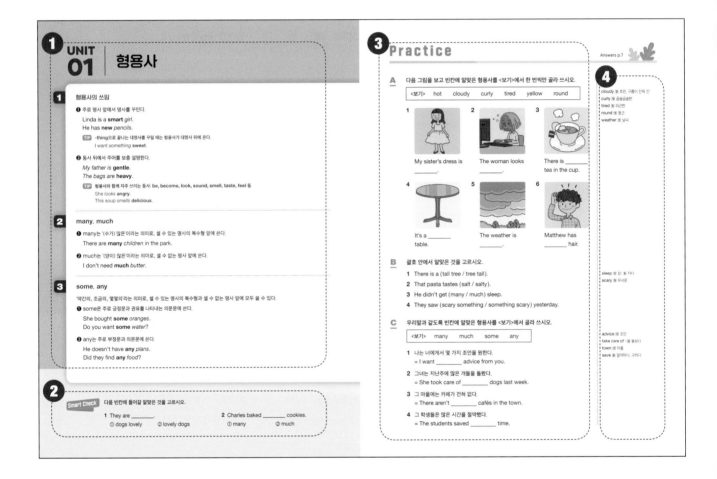

각 레벨에 딱 맞는
Essential Grammar Units

❶ Grammar Lesson

해당 레벨에서 익혀야 할 문법 개념을 명쾌한 설명과 실용적인 예문을 통해 정확하게 이해할 수 있습니다. TIP을 통해 내신 시험에서 출제되는 심화 문법까지 학습하여 고난도 문제에도 대비할 수 있습니다.

❸ Practice

다양한 유형의 풍부한 연습문제를 통해 문법 개념을 자연스럽게 이해할 수 있습니다.

❷ Smart Check

간단한 문제를 통해 위에서 배운 문법 개념을 잘 이해했는지 바로바로 확인할 수 있습니다.

❹ Vocabulary

연습문제에 쓰인 주요 어휘를 추가로 학습하여 어휘력까지 높일 수 있습니다.

*어휘 정리에 사용된 약호
명 명사   동 동사   형 형용사   부 부사   전 전치사   접 접속사

기초부터 실전까지 Perfect하게 완성 ────────────

기초를 탄탄히 다지는
기초 문법

중학영문법을 이해하기 위해 꼭 알아야 하는 기초 문법이 정리되어 있어, 문법 실력이 부족한 학생들도 기초를 탄탄히 다지고 본학습을 시작할 수 있습니다.

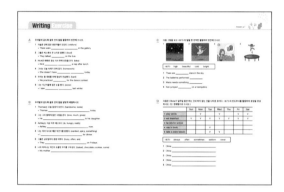

쓰기 활동으로 문법을 체득하는
Writing Exercise

다양한 유형의 서술형 문제를 풀어보며 쓰기 연습을 충분히 할 수 있습니다. 이를 통해 서술형을 강조하는 최근 내신 평가 트렌드에 대비할 수 있습니다.

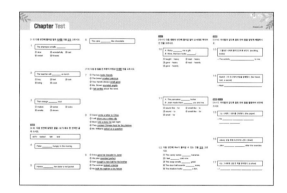

문제 풀이로 학습 내용을 확실히 점검하는
Chapter Test

전국 내신 기출문제 출제 유형을 기반으로 한 다양한 문제를 풀어보며 실제 시험에 대비할 수 있습니다. 서술형 주관식 문제 및 고난도 문제로 학습한 문법 개념에 대한 이해도를 점검할 수 있습니다.

학습 효과를 더욱 높이는
Workbook

각 UNIT별, Chapter별로 풍부한 양의 추가 문제를 풀면서 본교재에서 익힌 문법 개념을 확실히 복습하고 부족한 부분은 보완할 수 있습니다.

해커스북 중·고등

www.HackersBook.com

기초 문법

영어 문법, 그 기초부터 알고 들어가자!

1 영어 단어의 8가지 종류

영어 단어는 기능과 성격에 따라 **명사, 대명사, 동사, 형용사, 부사, 전치사, 접속사, 감탄사**로 분류할 수 있으며, 이를 품사라고 한다.

❶ 명사

명사는 **우리 주위에 있는 모든 것이 가지고 있는 이름**이다. 사람, 사물, 장소뿐만 아니라 눈에 보이지 않는 것들도 이름을 가지고 있다.

Jake, teacher, pencil, bed, bank, Korea, love, beauty 등

❷ 대명사

대명사는 **명사를 대신해서 쓰는 말**이다. 예를 들어 Jake는 he로, pencil은 it으로 대신해서 쓸 수 있다.

I, you, she, it, they, this, that 등

❸ 동사

동사는 **사람, 동물, 사물 등의 동작이나 상태를 나타내는 말**이다.

sleep, study, move, look, think, have 등

❹ 형용사

형용사는 **명사나 대명사를 꾸며 형태, 성질, 상태 등을 나타내는 말**이다.

long, round, cold, smart, new, funny 등

❺ 부사

부사는 **동사, 형용사, 다른 부사, 또는 문장 전체를 꾸미는 말**이다.

softly, quietly, really, hard, never, very 등

❻ 전치사

전치사는 **명사나 대명사 앞에서 장소나 시간 등을 나타내는 말**이다.

at, in, on, next to, during, with 등

❼ 접속사

접속사는 **말과 말을 연결해주는 말**이다.

and, but, or, when, because 등

❽ 감탄사

감탄사는 **기쁨, 놀람, 슬픔과 같은 다양한 감정을 표현하는 말**이다.

Oh, Wow, Bravo, Ouch

Check-up 다음 단어들에 해당되는 품사를 쓰시오.

1 hot, yellow, lovely	[ ]		**5** listen, drink, want	[ ]
2 loudly, usually, fast	[ ]		**6** but, when, because	[ ]
3 boy, bag, happiness	[ ]		**7** he, we, this	[ ]
4 on, behind, for	[ ]		**8** Oh, Wow, Oops	[ ]

정답 1 형용사 2 부사 3 명사 4 전치사 5 동사 6 접속사 7 대명사 8 감탄사

2 영어 문장을 만드는 재료

영어 문장을 만드는 여러 가지 재료로 **주어, 동사, 목적어, 보어, 수식어**가 있으며, 이를 **문장의 성분**이라고 한다.

❶ 주어
주어는 동작이나 상태의 주체가 되는 말로, '누가, 무엇이'에 해당한다.
The airplane flies fast.

❷ 동사
동사는 주어의 동작이나 상태를 나타내는 말로, '~하다, ~이다'에 해당한다.
The girl **sings** beautifully.

❸ 목적어
목적어는 동작의 대상이 되는 말로, '~을/를, ~에게'에 해당한다.
The students studied **math**.
I wrote **James a letter**.

❹ 보어
보어는 주어나 목적어를 보충 설명하는 말이다.
His mom is **a doctor**. <주격 보어>
The movie made me **sad**. <목적격 보어>

❺ 수식어
수식어는 문장에 반드시 필요하지는 않지만 다양한 위치에서 **여러 가지 의미를 더해주는 말**이다.
Jenny can jump **high**.
That is a **colorful** umbrella.

Check-up 다음 밑줄 친 부분의 문장 성분을 쓰시오.

1 I will go to the library <u>tomorrow</u>. [   ]

2 She <u>eats</u> salad every morning. [   ]

3 My brother likes <u>animals</u>. [   ]

4 <u>Chris</u> plays soccer after school. [   ]

5 The man is <u>a police officer</u>. [   ]

Chapter

01

명사

명사는 사람, 사물, 장소, 개념 등의 이름을 나타내는 말이다.

UNIT 01 | 셀 수 있는 명사

1 명사

❶ 사람, 사물, 장소, 개념 등의 이름을 나타내는 말이다.

John, girl, cup, pencil, store, Korea, love, friendship 등

❷ 하나, 둘 등으로 셀 수 있는 명사와 셀 수 없는 명사로 구분할 수 있다.

셀 수 있는 명사	boy, student, tiger, bird, map, car, country 등
셀 수 없는 명사	France, Seoul, love, health, water, juice 등

2 셀 수 있는 명사의 단수형

셀 수 있는 명사 하나를 나타낼 때는 명사 앞에 a(n)을 붙인다. 첫소리가 자음으로 발음되는 단어 앞에는 a를 쓰고, 첫소리가 모음으로 발음되는 단어 앞에는 an을 쓴다.

a + 첫소리가 자음으로 발음되는 단어	**a** teacher, **a** cat, **a** house, **a** week, **a** university 등
an + 첫소리가 모음으로 발음되는 단어	**an** artist, **an** egg, **an** idea, **an** hour 등

3 셀 수 있는 명사의 복수형

셀 수 있는 명사 둘 이상을 나타낼 때는 복수형으로 쓴다. 셀 수 있는 명사의 복수형은 대부분 명사에 -(e)s를 붙여 만들며, 일부는 불규칙하게 변한다.

대부분의 명사	명사 + -s	desk – desk**s**	tree – tree**s**
-s, -x, -ch, -sh로 끝나는 명사	명사 + -es	bus – bus**es** watch – watch**es**	box – box**es** dish – dish**es**
「자음 + o」로 끝나는 명사	명사 + -es	potato – potato**es** ※ 예외: piano – piano**s**	tomato – tomato**es** photo – photo**s**
「자음 + y」로 끝나는 명사	y를 i로 바꾸고 + -es	baby – bab**ies**	lady – lad**ies**
-f, -fe로 끝나는 명사	f, fe를 v로 바꾸고 + -es	leaf – lea**ves** ※ 예외: roof – roof**s**	knife – kni**ves**
불규칙하게 변하는 명사	man – **men** mouse – **mice**	woman – **women** tooth – **teeth**	child – **children** foot – **feet**
단수형과 복수형이 같은 명사	sheep – **sheep**	deer – **deer**	fish – **fish**

The **children** have small **bags**.

Smart Check 밑줄 친 부분이 어법상 맞으면 O를 쓰고, 틀리면 X를 쓰시오.

1 <u>an</u> apple → _____

2 <u>a</u> umbrella → _____

3 three <u>stories</u> → _____

4 four <u>man</u> → _____

Practice

Answers p.2

A 다음 빈칸에 a와 an 중 알맞은 것을 쓰시오.

1	_____ student	**7**	_____ rabbit
2	_____ eraser	**8**	_____ truck
3	_____ table	**9**	_____ island
4	_____ animal	**10**	_____ girl
5	_____ dolphin	**11**	_____ actor
6	_____ hour	**12**	_____ week

eraser 몡 지우개
animal 몡 동물
dolphin 몡 돌고래
island 몡 섬
actor 몡 배우

B 다음 명사의 복수형을 쓰시오.

1	bird – _____	**7**	pen – _____
2	church – _____	**8**	city – _____
3	thief – _____	**9**	photo – _____
4	party – _____	**10**	foot – _____
5	fish – _____	**11**	fox – _____
6	potato – _____	**12**	wish – _____

church 몡 교회
thief 몡 도둑
city 몡 도시
fox 몡 여우
wish 몡 소원

C 괄호 안의 명사를 알맞은 형태로 바꿔 빈칸에 쓰시오.

1 I have a _____. (doll)

2 There are five _____. (wolf)

3 She needs a _____. (map)

4 There are six _____. (box)

5 They want an _____. (orange)

6 The man has four _____. (sheep)

7 Ms. Davis has three _____. (child)

8 He eats two _____ every week. (tomato)

doll 몡 인형
wolf 몡 늑대
need 동 필요하다
want 동 원하다

UNIT 02 | 셀 수 없는 명사

1 셀 수 없는 명사의 종류

❶ 사람, 국가, 도시 등의 고유한 이름을 나타내는 명사

Alice, Mr. Smith, Italy, Beijing, Jejudo 등

❷ 추상적인 개념을 나타내는 명사

love, peace, hope, help, health, honesty, happiness 등

❸ 일정한 형태가 없는 물질을 나타내는 명사

water, oil, milk, sugar, bread, rice, paper, money 등

2 셀 수 없는 명사의 수

❶ 셀 수 없는 명사는 항상 단수 취급하며, 명사 앞에 a(n)을 붙일 수 없고 복수형으로도 쓸 수 없다.

Leo lives in **Seattle**.
They have **hope**.
She wants **bread**.

❷ 셀 수 없는 명사는 그것을 담는 그릇이나 단위를 나타내는 말인 단위명사를 활용하여 수량을 나타내고, 복수형은 단위명사에 -(e)s 를 붙여 만든다.

잔	**a glass of** water/milk/juice
컵/잔	**a cup of** tea/coffee
병	**a bottle of** water/juice
그릇	**a bowl of** soup/rice
조각	**a slice[piece] of** pizza/cheese/bread/cake
장	**a piece of** paper

I drink **a cup of** *tea* at night.
He eats **two bowls of** *soup* in the morning.
We need **four pieces of** *paper*.

Smart Check 밑줄 친 부분이 어법상 맞으면 O를 쓰고, 틀리면 X를 쓰시오.

1 a health → _____
2 Seouls → _____
3 peace → _____
4 three glass of milk → _____
5 a slice of cake → _____
6 two bottles of waters → _____

Practice

Answers p.2

A 다음 명사가 셀 수 있는 명사이면 O, 셀 수 없는 명사이면 X를 쓰시오.

1 love → _____
6 pencil → _____
2 book → _____
7 friendship → _____
3 Paris → _____
8 finger → _____
4 oil → _____
9 melon → _____
5 salt → _____
10 Justin → _____

book 명 책
salt 명 소금
pencil 명 연필
friendship 명 우정
finger 명 손가락
melon 명 멜론

B 괄호 안에서 알맞은 것을 고르시오.

1 He has (money / moneys).
2 We want (an honesty / honesty) from you.
3 (A Daniel / Daniel) is from Germany.
4 The country needs (peace / peaces).
5 I eat two pieces of (bread / breads) for dinner.
6 Nicole drinks (a water / a glass of water) after meals.

country 명 나라
dinner 명 (저녁) 식사
meal 명 식사

C 다음 그림을 보고 <보기>와 같이 괄호 안의 말을 활용하여 빈칸을 완성하시오.

<보기>

two cups of tea
(cup, tea)

1

_____
(bottle, juice)

2

_____
(piece, paper)

3

_____
(bowl, rice)

4

_____
(glass, milk)

5

_____
(slice, pizza)

Chapter 01 명사 **15**

Chapter 01

명사

Hackers Grammar Smart Starter

Writing Exercise

A 우리말과 같도록 괄호 안의 명사를 활용하여 영작하시오.

1 학생 세 명 (student) = _____

2 도시 네 개 (city) = _____

3 남자 여섯 명 (man) = _____

4 개미 한 마리 (ant) = _____

5 치즈 두 조각 (cheese) = _____

6 피아노 열 대 (piano) = _____

7 일주일 (week) = _____

8 쿠키 다섯 개 (cookie) = _____

9 종이 세 장 (paper) = _____

B 우리말과 같도록 괄호 안의 명사를 활용하여 문장을 완성하시오.

1 나는 강아지들을 좋아한다. (puppy)

= I like _____.

2 나무 위에 올빼미 한 마리가 있다. (owl)

= There is _____ on the tree.

3 우정은 그에게 중요하다. (friendship)

= _____ is important to him.

4 한 시간에는 60분이 있다. (hour)

= There are 60 minutes in _____.

5 그녀는 매일 아침 커피 한 잔을 마신다. (coffee)

= She drinks _____ every morning.

6 축구는 유럽에서 인기 있다. (Europe)

= Soccer is popular in _____.

C 다음 그림을 보고 <보기>와 같이 괄호 안의 명사를 활용하여 문장을 완성하시오. (단, 단위명사를 쓰지 마시오.)

<보기>	I have _two fish_ . (fish)

1 I have _____. (egg)

2 I have _____. (watermelon)

3 I have _____. (milk)

4 I have _____. (peach)

5 I have _____. (bread)

D 다음 그림을 보고 괄호 안의 명사를 활용하여 빈칸에 쓰시오.

1 There are _____ _____ in the room. (woman)

2 There are _____ _____ on the table. (candle)

3 There are _____ _____ on the table. (knife)

4 There are _____ _____ on the table. (dish)

5 There is _____ _____ _____ _____ on the table. (water)

6 Chloe drinks _____ _____ _____ _____ _____. (orange juice)

7 Amanda eats _____ _____ _____ _____. (bread)

8 Emma eats _____ _____ _____ _____. (pizza)

Chapter Test

[1-2] 다음 중 명사의 복수형이 <u>잘못된</u> 것을 고르시오.

1 ① class – classes ② lady – ladies
   ③ tooth – teeth ④ movie – movies
   ⑤ leaf – leafes

2 ① deer – deers ② tomato – tomatoes
   ③ photo – photos ④ woman – women
   ⑤ city – cities

3 다음 중 명사의 종류가 나머지 넷과 <u>다른</u> 것은?

   ① rain ② honesty ③ Mr. Carlson
   ④ kindness ⑤ country

[4-5] 다음 중 밑줄 친 부분이 어법상 <u>어색한</u> 것을 고르시오.

4 ① There is <u>a</u> boy in the room.
   ② <u>A</u> window is open.
   ③ Sophie has <u>an</u> orange.
   ④ We live in <u>a</u> apartment.
   ⑤ <u>An</u> eraser is under the desk.

5 ① We have three <u>dogs</u>.
   ② I need <u>help</u>.
   ③ George eats <u>a cucumber</u>.
   ④ There is <u>an egg</u> in the bowl.
   ⑤ Ms. Wilson puts <u>a sugar</u> in her coffee.

6 다음 빈칸에 들어갈 말이 나머지 넷과 <u>다른</u> 것은?

   ① _____ week has seven days.
   ② He is _____ great architect.
   ③ There is _____ umbrella at the door.
   ④ Carl is _____ university student.
   ⑤ _____ chair is next to the desk.

[7-8] 괄호 안의 말을 활용하여 문장을 완성하시오.

7
> There are ten _____ in the basket.
> (potato)

8
> My grandmother drinks two _____
> in the afternoon. (cup, tea)

[9-10] 다음 빈칸에 들어갈 말로 <u>어색한</u> 것을 고르시오.

9
> Jake wants a _____.

   ① pencil ② notebooks ③ map
   ④ computer ⑤ dictionary

10
> _____ is important.

   ① Water ② Happiness ③ Health
   ④ Friend ⑤ Peace

[11-12] 다음 중 어법상 <u>어색한</u> 것을 고르시오.

11 ① I have funny photos.
② My parents give love to me.
③ Marie has two brothers.
④ There is a slide in the playground.
⑤ They are cute babys.

12 ① Horses eat carrots.
② Dad drinks coffees every day.
③ There is hope for the future.
④ My friend lives in China.
⑤ There is a piece of cheese in my sandwich.

고난도
[13-14] 다음 빈칸에 들어갈 말이 순서대로 짝지어진 것을 고르시오. (단, X는 필요 없음을 의미함)

13
• There are four glasses of _____ on the table.
• Mr. Hill needs _____ idea for his story.

① water – a   ② water – an   ③ water – X
④ waters – a   ⑤ waters – an

14
• Sarah is from _____ Sydney.
• There are five _____ in the fish tank.

① X – fish   ② a – fish   ③ X – fishs
④ a – fishes   ⑤ X – fishes

서술형
[15-16] 다음 문장에서 어법상 <u>어색한</u> 부분을 찾아 쓰고 바르게 고쳐 쓰시오.

15
There are watchs in the box.

_____ → _____

16
Tiffany wants two bottles of juices.

_____ → _____

서술형 고난도
[17-20] 우리말과 같도록 괄호 안의 명사를 활용하여 문장을 완성하시오.

17
그 고양이들은 매일 쥐들을 잡는다. (mouse)

= The cats catch _____ every day.

18
나는 점심 식사를 위해 돈이 필요하다. (money)

= I need _____ for lunch.

19
접시 위에 빵 두 조각이 있다. (bread)

= There are _____ on the plate.

20
들판에 양 두 마리와 아이들 세 명이 있다. (sheep, child)

= There are _____ and _____ in the field.

Chapter 01

명사

Hackers Grammar Smart Starter

Word Review

Chapter 01에 나온 어휘 중 잘 외워지지 않는 것은 박스에 체크하여 복습하시오.

☐ friendship	몡 우정	☐ important	톙 중요한
☐ country	몡 나라	☐ popular	톙 인기 있는
☐ hour	몡 시간	☐ watermelon	몡 수박
☐ island	몡 섬	☐ kindness	몡 친절
☐ church	몡 교회	☐ live	톰 살다
☐ thief	몡 도둑	☐ apartment	몡 아파트
☐ wish	몡 소원; 톰 바라다	☐ architect	몡 건축가
☐ need	톰 필요하다	☐ university	몡 대학교
☐ want	톰 원하다	☐ dictionary	몡 사전
☐ peace	몡 평화	☐ funny	톙 웃긴
☐ hope	몡 희망	☐ playground	몡 운동장, 놀이터
☐ honesty	몡 정직	☐ fish tank	어항
☐ happiness	몡 행복	☐ catch	톰 잡다
☐ meal	몡 식사	☐ plate	몡 접시
☐ owl	몡 올빼미	☐ field	몡 들판

Check-up

영어 어휘와 알맞은 우리말 뜻을 연결하시오.

1	country	•	• ⓐ 희망	6	meal	•	• ⓐ 인기 있는
2	dictionary	•	• ⓑ 나라	7	popular	•	• ⓑ 도둑
3	hope	•	• ⓒ 필요하다	8	field	•	• ⓒ 들판
4	need	•	• ⓓ 정직	9	thief	•	• ⓓ 중요한
5	honesty	•	• ⓔ 사전	10	important	•	• ⓔ 식사

정답 1 ⓑ 2 ⓔ 3 ⓐ 4 ⓒ 5 ⓓ 6 ⓔ 7 ⓐ 8 ⓒ 9 ⓑ 10 ⓓ

Chapter

02

대명사

대명사는 앞에서 언급된 특정한 명사를 반복하지 않기 위해
대신해서 쓰는 말이다.

UNIT 01 | 인칭대명사

1 대명사

대명사는 앞에서 언급된 특정한 명사를 반복하지 않기 위해 대신해서 쓰는 말이다.

Susan is healthy. **She** exercises every day.

2 인칭대명사

인칭대명사는 사람이나 사물의 이름을 대신하는 말로, 인칭·수·격에 따라 형태가 다르다.

인칭·수	격	주격	소유격	목적격
1인칭	단수	I	my	me
	복수	we	our	us
2인칭	단수·복수	you	your	you
3인칭	단수	he	his	him
		she	her	her
		it	its	it
	복수	they	their	them

❶ 주격 인칭대명사(~은/는, ~이/가)는 문장의 주어 역할을 한다.

I am tall.
We are students.

❷ 소유격 인칭대명사(~의)는 명사 앞에서 소유 관계를 나타낸다.

Jack is **my** *brother*.
She has **your** *umbrella*.

> **TIP** 사람을 나타내는 명사의 소유격은 명사에 -'s를 붙여 만들며, -s로 끝나는 복수명사에는 -'만 붙여 만든다.
> **Helen's** *shoes* are pretty.
> They are the **singers'** *fans*.

❸ 목적격 인칭대명사(~을/를, ~에게)는 동사나 전치사의 목적어 역할을 한다.

Mom *loves* **us**.
The book is difficult *for* **him**.

Smart Check 다음 빈칸에 들어갈 알맞은 것을 고르시오.

1 _____ is a pianist.

① He ② His

2 They are _____ parents.

① me ② my

Practice

Answers p.3

A 다음 말을 알맞은 주격 인칭대명사로 바꿔 쓰시오.

1 William → _____

2 a bear → _____

3 Julia → _____

4 you and Kathy → _____

5 the kids → _____

6 my mother → _____

7 Tom and I → _____

8 a doll → _____

9 Mr. Blair → _____

10 five roses → _____

bear 몡 곰
kid 몡 아이
doll 몡 인형
rose 몡 장미

B 괄호 안에서 알맞은 것을 고르시오.

1 I have (it / its) now.

2 He knows (I / my) address.

3 (Alex's / Alex) story is sad.

4 Betty likes (she / her) dog.

5 I always think about (you / your).

6 (We / Us) are in the same class.

now 뫼 지금
know 동 알다, 알고 있다
address 몡 주소
always 뫼 항상
think about ~에 대해 생각하다
same 혱 같은

C 우리말과 같도록 괄호 안의 인칭대명사를 알맞은 형태로 바꿔 빈칸에 쓰시오.

1 (he)

① 그는 반장이다. = _____ is the class president.

② 나는 그의 전화번호를 가지고 있다. = I have _____ phone number.

2 (they)

① 그들의 노래는 인기 있다. = _____ songs are popular.

② Jake는 TV에서 그들을 본다. = Jake sees _____ on TV.

3 (you)

① Sarah는 너를 아주 그리워한다. = Sarah really misses _____.

② 그녀는 너의 편지를 기다린다. = She waits for _____ letters.

4 (we)

① 우리는 운동을 잘한다. = _____ are good at sports.

② 나는 우리를 정말 자랑스러워한다. = I am so proud of _____.

class president 반장
popular 혱 인기 있는
wait for ~을 기다리다
good at ~을 잘하는
so 뫼 정말, 너무나
proud of ~을 자랑스러워 하는

UNIT 02 | this, that, it

1 this

❶ '이 사람, 이것'이라는 의미로 가까이 있는 사람이나 사물을 가리킬 때 쓰며, 복수형은 these이다.

This is my sister.
These are new computers.

❷ this와 these는 '이 ~'라는 의미로 명사 앞에서 명사를 꾸밀 수 있다.

This *mango* is sweet.
These *boys* are smart.

2 that

❶ '저 사람, 저것'이라는 의미로 멀리 있는 사람이나 사물을 가리킬 때 쓰며, 복수형은 those이다.

That is Carol's friend.
Those are our books.

❷ that과 those는 '저 ~'라는 의미로 명사 앞에서 명사를 꾸밀 수 있다.

He likes **that** *restaurant*.
Those *children* want chocolate.

3 비인칭 주어 it

날씨, 계절, 시간, 요일, 날짜, 명암, 거리를 나타낼 때 문장의 주어로 쓰며, 해석하지 않는다.

It is rainy today. <날씨>
It is autumn now. <계절>
It is 10 P.M. <시간>
It is Sunday. <요일>
It is May 5 today. <날짜>
It is bright outside. <명암>
It is 30 meters to the station. <거리>

Smart Check 다음 빈칸에 들어갈 알맞은 것을 고르시오.

1 _____ dogs are small.
　① This　　　② These

2 _____ is Friday today.
　① That　　　② It

Practice

Answers p.3

A 괄호 안에서 알맞은 것을 고르시오.

1 (That / Those) is his house.

2 (This / These) are your textbooks.

3 (This / It) is cloudy now.

4 The baby likes (that / those) toys.

5 (This / These) is my neighbor John.

textbook 몡 교과서
cloudy 혱 흐린, 구름이 잔뜩 낀
toy 몡 장난감
neighbor 몡 이웃

B 다음 그림을 보고 빈칸에 알맞은 말을 <보기>에서 골라 쓰시오.

<보기>	this	these	that	those	it

funny 혱 재미있는, 웃기는
comic book 만화책
ear 몡 귀
July 몡 7월
fire station 소방서

1 _____ is 10:30 now.

2 _____ flowers are beautiful.

3 _____ are funny comic books.

4 _____ rabbit has big ears.

5 _____ is July 4 today.

6 _____ is a fire station.

C 우리말과 같도록 빈칸에 알맞은 말을 쓰시오.

1 그녀는 저 컴퓨터를 사용한다.   = She uses _____ computer.

2 밤에는 어둡다.   = _____ is dark at night.

3 이것은 그의 자리이다.   = _____ is his seat.

4 이 사람들은 나의 반 친구들이다.   = _____ are my classmates.

dark 혱 어두운
night 몡 밤
seat 몡 자리, 좌석
classmate 몡 반 친구

Writing Exercise

A 다음 문장의 밑줄 친 부분을 알맞은 인칭대명사로 바꿔 빈칸에 쓰시오. (단, 인칭대명사의 격에 주의하시오.)

1 <u>Judy</u> is very friendly. I like _____.

2 There is <u>an elephant</u>. _____ nose is long.

3 <u>Mr. Brown</u> is an English teacher. _____ is Australian.

4 I love <u>the movie</u>. I watch _____ every year.

5 <u>The children</u> are in the playground. _____ parents are on a bench.

6 <u>Julie and I</u> meet Matt every morning. He walks to school with _____.

7 <u>Anna and Emma</u> are twins. _____ share the same room.

B 우리말과 같도록 빈칸에 알맞은 말을 쓰시오.

1 저 오리들은 빠르게 헤엄친다. = _____ ducks swim fast.

2 지금은 오전 8시다. = _____ is 8 A.M. now.

3 이 자전거는 새것이다. = _____ bicycle is new.

4 이 사람들은 나의 사촌들이다. = _____ are my cousins.

5 저것은 훌륭한 그림이다. = _____ is a great picture.

6 오늘은 바람이 많이 분다. = _____ is windy today.

7 이것은 우체국이다. = _____ is a post office.

8 이 소년들은 Sam과 Bart이다. = _____ boys are Sam and Bart.

C 우리말과 같도록 괄호 안의 말을 알맞게 배열하시오.

1 저것은 단풍나무이다. (a maple tree, is, that)

= _____.

2 이것들은 오래된 동전들이다. (old coins, are, these)

= _____.

3 그녀의 소설은 인기 있다. (popular, novel, her, is)

= _____.

4 이 남자분은 나의 축구 코치이시다. (soccer coach, this, my, is, man)

= _____.

5 그의 새 교복은 편하다. (is, his, comfortable, new school uniform)

= _____.

6 행복은 나에게 중요하다. (important, is, to me, happiness)

= _____.

D 다음 그림을 보고 빈칸에 알맞은 말을 <보기>에서 한 번씩만 골라 쓰시오.

| <보기> | my | we | their | them | these | those | it |

1 _____ is summer.

2 _____ family is at the beach. I am on the sunbed.

3 _____ are my sunglasses. I always bring _____ to the beach.

4 _____ are my parents. _____ swimsuits are purple.

5 _____ are very happy now.

Chapter Test

[1-2] 다음 빈칸에 들어갈 알맞은 것을 고르시오.

1

| _____ is 9:30 in the morning. |

① This   ② That   ③ It
④ These   ⑤ Those

2

| There are five children. _____ look sleepy. |

① I   ② We   ③ He
④ They   ⑤ You

[3-4] 다음 빈칸에 들어갈 말로 <u>어색한</u> 것을 고르시오.

3

| That is _____ jacket. |

① my   ② your   ③ her
④ Kate's   ⑤ him

4

| The noodles are too spicy for _____. |

① me   ② our   ③ her
④ you   ⑤ them

[5-6] 다음 두 문장의 의미가 같도록 빈칸에 알맞은 말을 쓰시오.

5

| Beth and I live in the same town. → _____ live in the same town. |

6

| That is my brother's homework. → That is _____ homework. |

[7-9] 다음 중 밑줄 친 부분이 어법상 <u>어색한</u> 것을 고르시오.

7 ① <u>She</u> likes cucumbers.
② <u>Our</u> classroom is on the second floor.
③ George talks to <u>their</u>.
④ <u>It</u> is dark in the evening.
⑤ <u>His</u> sister cooks delicious potato soup.

8 ① <u>This</u> is my smartphone.
② <u>Those</u> are their credit cards.
③ <u>These</u> windows are clean.
④ <u>That</u> cheetah runs very fast.
⑤ <u>This</u> clocks are old.

9 ① <u>Their</u> house is at the corner.
② <u>This</u> is October 29 today.
③ Jackson has lunch with <u>his</u> parents.
④ Those are for <u>you</u>.
⑤ She calls <u>me</u> every night.

서술형 **고난도**

[10-12] 괄호 안의 말을 활용하여 문장을 완성하시오.

10
_____ chair is new. (the teacher)

11
Mr. Nelson bakes cookies. He gives _____ to us. (they)

12
I listen to _____ songs every day. (she)

13 다음 빈칸에 공통으로 들어갈 알맞은 것은?

• _____ is fall now.
• Erica has a bicycle. _____ is heavy.

① This   ② That   ③ It
④ She   ⑤ They

14 다음 대화의 빈칸에 들어갈 알맞은 것은?

A: Is _____ your house over there ?
B: Yes. I live there.

① that   ② these   ③ those
④ they   ⑤ them

고난도

15 다음 중 밑줄 친 it의 쓰임이 나머지 넷과 다른 것은?

① It is bright in the kitchen.
② It is 10 P.M. in England now.
③ It is my notebook.
④ It is five kilometers to school.
⑤ It is Tuesday.

서술형

[16-18] 우리말과 같도록 빈칸에 알맞은 말을 쓰시오.

16
오늘은 화창하다.

= _____ is sunny today.

17
저 담요들은 따뜻하다.

= _____ blankets are warm.

18
나는 매일 아침 그와 함께 조깅한다.

= _____ jog with _____ every morning.

서술형

19 다음 대화에서 어법상 어색한 부분을 찾아 쓰고 바르게 고쳐 쓰시오.

A: Wow, these watermelon is sweet.
B: Yes. It is very delicious.

_____ → _____

Word Review

Chapter 02에 나온 어휘 중 잘 외워지지 않는 것은 박스에 체크하여 복습하시오.

□ exercise	동 운동하다	□ cloudy	형 흐린, 구름이 잔뜩 낀
□ pretty	형 예쁜	□ neighbor	명 이웃
□ difficult	형 어려운	□ beautiful	형 아름다운
□ pianist	명 피아니스트	□ fire station	소방서
□ address	명 주소	□ dark	형 어두운
□ class president	반장	□ seat	명 자리, 좌석
□ wait for	~을 기다리다	□ classmate	명 반 친구
□ good at	~을 잘하는	□ walk	동 걷다
□ proud of	~을 자랑스러워하는	□ twin	명 쌍둥이
□ rainy	형 비가 오는	□ share	동 함께 쓰다, 공유하다
□ autumn	명 가을	□ cousin	명 사촌
□ bright	형 밝은	□ beach	명 해변
□ outside	부 밖에, 밖에서	□ spicy	형 매운
□ station	명 역	□ blanket	명 담요
□ textbook	명 교과서	□ delicious	형 맛있는

Check-up

영어 어휘와 알맞은 우리말 뜻을 연결하시오.

1 address · · ⓐ 함께 쓰다, 공유하다
2 good at · · ⓑ 주소
3 share · · ⓒ 맛있는
4 delicious · · ⓓ ~을 잘하는
5 outside · · ⓔ 밖에, 밖에서

6 difficult · · ⓐ 운동하다
7 exercise · · ⓑ 어려운
8 wait for · · ⓒ 역
9 station · · ⓓ 걷다
10 walk · · ⓔ ~을 기다리다

Chapter

03

be동사

be동사는 주어의 상태를 나타내는 동사로,
나타내는 시점과 주어에 따라 형태가 달라진다.

UNIT 01 | be동사의 현재형

1 be동사

주어의 상태를 나타내는 동사로, '~이다, ~(하)다, (~에) 있다'의 의미이다.

I **am** a singer.
Adam **is** tall.
We **are** in the library.

2 be동사의 현재형

❶ be동사의 현재형은 주어의 인칭과 수에 따라 am/are/is를 쓴다.

인칭	수	주어(인칭대명사)	be동사의 현재형
1인칭	단수	I	am
	복수	We	are
2인칭	단수·복수	You	are
3인칭	단수	He / She / It	is
	복수	They	are

I **am** at a restaurant.
You **are** healthy.
He **is** a nurse.

❷ 주어가 인칭대명사인 경우 「주어 + be동사」를 줄여 쓸 수 있다.

주어(인칭대명사) + be동사	줄임말
I am	I'm
We are	We're
You are	You're
He is / She is / It is	He's / She's / It's
They are	They're

I'm busy.
We're at school.
It's my phone.

Smart Check 다음 빈칸에 들어갈 알맞은 것을 고르시오.

1 He _____ my classmate.

　① is 　　　② are

2 _____ in the living room.

　① They's 　② They're

Practice

Answers p.4

A 괄호 안에서 알맞은 것을 고르시오.

1 I (am / is) hungry now.

2 He (is / are) in Canada now.

3 We (am / are) in the car.

4 Her mother (is / are) a cook.

5 Chris and Emma (is / are) middle school students.

hungry 형 배고픈
cook 명 요리사
middle school 중학교
student 명 학생

B 다음 문장의 밑줄 친 부분을 줄여 쓰시오.

1 He is a great doctor. → _____

2 You are handsome. → _____

3 They are at the aquarium. → _____

4 She is sick. → _____

5 I am at the park. → _____

6 We are lucky today. → _____

7 It is a bear. → _____

great 형 훌륭한
doctor 명 의사
handsome 형 멋진, 잘생긴
aquarium 명 수족관
sick 형 아픈
lucky 형 운이 좋은

C 다음 그림을 보고 빈칸에 알맞은 be동사의 현재형을 쓰시오.

1

I _____ good at math.

2

She _____ a pilot.

3

They _____ from Germany.

math 명 수학
pilot 명 조종사
Germany 명 독일
firefighter 명 소방관
train 명 기차
fast 형 빠른

4

Mr. Jones _____ a firefighter.

5

This train _____ fast.

6

The monkeys _____ on the tree.

1 ### be동사 현재형의 부정문

「주어 + be동사의 현재형 + not」의 형태로 '~이 아니다, ~(하)지 않다, (~에) 있지 않다'의 의미이며, 줄여 쓸 수 있다.

주어(인칭대명사)	be동사의 현재형 + not	줄임말	
I	am not	I'm not	
He		He's not	He isn't
She	is not	She's not	She isn't
It		It's not	It isn't
We		We're not	We aren't
You	are not	You're not	You aren't
They		They're not	They aren't

He's not honest.　　　　　**They aren't** in the classroom.

TIP **I am not**은 **I'm not**으로만 줄여 쓴다.
(~~I amn't~~, **I'm not**) ready.

- -

2 ### be동사 현재형의 의문문

「be동사의 현재형 + 주어 ~?」의 형태로, '~이니?, ~(하)니?, (~에) 있니?'의 의미이다. 긍정의 대답은 「Yes, 주어 + be동사의 현재형.」, 부정의 대답은 「No, 주어 + be동사의 현재형 + not.」의 형태이다.

인칭	수	be동사 현재형의 의문문	긍정의 대답	부정의 대답
1인칭	단수	Am I ~?	Yes, you are.	No, you aren't.
	복수	Are we ~?	Yes, we/you are.	No, we/you aren't.
2인칭	단수	Are you ~?	Yes, I am.	No, I'm not.
	복수	Are you ~?	Yes, we are.	No, we aren't.
3인칭	단수	Is he/she/it ~?	Yes, he/she/it is.	No, he/she/it isn't.
	복수	Are they ~?	Yes, they are.	No, they aren't.

A: **Are you** thirsty?　　　*B:* **Yes, I am. / No, I'm not.**

TIP 긍정의 대답에서 **Yes** 뒤에 오는 「주어 + be동사」는 줄여 쓰지 않는다.
Yes, I'm. (X)　　　Yes, we're. (X)　　　Yes, she's. (X)

Smart Check 다음 빈칸에 들어갈 알맞은 것을 고르시오.

1 We _____ teachers.
　① are not　　② not are

2 _____ it cheap?
　① Are　　② Is

Practice

Answers p.4

A 괄호 안에서 알맞은 것을 고르시오.

1 (I'm not / I amn't) lonely.

2 She (is not / not is) a writer.

3 (Is / Are) you a pianist?

4 (Is / Am) the cat in the box?

5 We (isn't / aren't) angry.

6 *A*: Is this your backpack?
  B: No, it (is / isn't).

lonely 형 외로운
writer 명 작가
pianist 명 피아니스트
angry 형 화난
backpack 명 배낭

B 다음 문장의 밑줄 친 부분을 줄여 쓰시오.

1 I am not weak. → _____

2 You are not noisy. → _____

3 It is not windy today. → _____

4 He is not a rude boy. → _____

5 They are not at the bank. → _____

weak 형 약한, 허약한
noisy 형 시끄러운
windy 형 바람이 많이 부는
rude 형 무례한

C 괄호 안의 말과 be동사의 현재형을 활용하여 대화를 완성하시오.

1 *A*: _____ _____ your water bottle? (it)
  B: No, _____ _____.

2 *A*: _____ _____ in the bathroom? (he)
  B: Yes, _____ _____.

3 *A*: _____ _____ _____ at the concert? (your sister)
  B: No, _____ _____.

4 *A*: _____ _____ _____ difficult? (the problems)
  B: No, _____ _____.

5 *A*: _____ _____ _____ _____ in the same class?
    (you and Edward)
  B: Yes, _____ _____.

water bottle 물병
bathroom 명 화장실
concert 명 연주회, 콘서트
difficult 형 어려운
problem 명 문제

UNIT 03 be동사의 과거형

1 be동사의 과거형

'~이었다, ~(했)다, (~에) 있었다'의 의미로, 주어에 따라 was나 were를 쓴다.

주어(인칭대명사)	be동사의 과거형
I / He / She / It	was
We / You / They	were

I **was** full.
We **were** at home yesterday.
→ 과거형은 yesterday, last night, an hour ago 등의 과거를 나타내는 표현과 주로 함께 쓰인다.

2 be동사 과거형의 부정문

「주어 + be동사의 과거형 + not」의 형태로 '~이 아니었다, ~(하)지 않았다, (~에) 있지 않았다'의 의미이며, 줄여 쓸 수 있다.

주어(인칭대명사)	be동사의 과거형 + not	줄임말
I / He / She / It	was not	wasn't
We / You / They	were not	weren't

She was not[wasn't] a dancer.
They were not[weren't] free.

3 be동사 과거형의 의문문

「be동사의 과거형 + 주어 ~?」의 형태로, '~이었니?, ~(했)니?, (~에) 있었니?'의 의미이다. 긍정의 대답은 「Yes, 주어 + be동사의 과거형.」, 부정의 대답은 「No, 주어 + be동사의 과거형 + not.」의 형태이다.

be동사 과거형의 의문문	긍정의 대답	부정의 대답
Was/Were + 주어 ~?	Yes, 주어 + was/were.	No, 주어 + wasn't/weren't.

A: **Was he** nervous? B: **Yes, he was. / No, he wasn't.**
A: **Were you** at the lake? B: **Yes, we were. / No, we weren't.**

Smart Check 다음 빈칸에 들어갈 알맞은 것을 고르시오.

1 They _____ hungry last night.
① were   ② was

2 I _____ in Incheon a month ago.
① wasn't   ② weren't

3 _____ it heavy?
① Was   ② Were

Practice

A 괄호 안에서 알맞은 것을 고르시오.

1 Jimmy (was / were) at school an hour ago.

2 We (wasn't / weren't) sure.

3 My friends (was / were) in the elevator.

4 She (was not / not was) a nurse.

5 (Was / Were) your brother at the gym?

6 A: (Was / Were) you tired last night?
    B: Yes, I (was / were).

sure 휑 확신하는, 확실한
elevator 몡 엘리베이터
nurse 몡 간호사
gym 몡 체육관
tired 휑 피곤한

B 다음 그림을 보고 be동사의 과거형을 활용하여 빈칸에 알맞은 말을 쓰시오. (단, 부정문에서는 줄임말을 쓰시오.)

1  2  3

science 몡 과학
classroom 몡 교실
playground 몡 놀이터, 운동장
funny 휑 웃기는
sad 휑 슬픈

1 Mr. Young _____ an English teacher. He _____ a science teacher.

2 The children _____ in the classroom. They _____ in the playground.

3 The movie _____ funny. It _____ sad.

C 괄호 안의 말과 be동사의 과거형을 활용하여 대화를 완성하시오.

1 A: _____ _____ at the festival yesterday? (they)
    B: No, _____ _____ .

2 A: _____ _____ _____ great? (the show)
    B: Yes, _____ _____ .

3 A: _____ _____ snowy last Sunday? (it)
    B: No, _____ _____ .

4 A: _____ _____ loud? (I)
    B: Yes, _____ _____ .

festival 몡 축제
snowy 휑 눈이 내리는
loud 휑 시끄러운

UNIT 04 | There + be동사

1 「There + be동사」의 의미와 형태

「There + be동사」는 '~이 있(었)다'라는 의미로, 뒤에 오는 명사의 수에 따라 be동사의 형태가 달라진다. 이때 There는 해석하지 않는다.

| There | + | is/was | + | 셀 수 있는 명사의 단수형 또는 셀 수 없는 명사 |
| | | are/were | | 셀 수 있는 명사의 복수형 |

There is *a man* in the room.
There was *water* on the floor.

There are *two cats* on the bench.
There were *four potatoes* in the basket.

2 「There + be동사」의 부정문

「There + be동사 + not」의 형태로, '~이 없(었)다'라는 의미이다.

There is not[isn't] much salt in the bottle.
There were not[weren't] ducks in the pond.

3 「There + be동사」의 의문문

「be동사 + there ~?」의 형태로, '~이 있(었)니?'라는 의미이다. 긍정의 대답은 「Yes, there + be동사.」, 부정의 대답은 「No, there + be동사 + not.」의 형태이다.

A: **Is there** a ruler on the desk?
B: **Yes, there is. / No, there isn't.**

A: **Was there** sand in your shoes?
B: **Yes, there was. / No, there wasn't.**

Smart Check 다음 빈칸에 들어갈 알맞은 것을 고르시오.

1 There _____ a painting on the wall.
　① is　　　　　② are

2 There _____ much milk in the cup.
　① wasn't　　　② weren't

3 _____ there many stars in the sky?
　① Was　　　　② Were

Practice

Answers p.4

A 괄호 안에서 알맞은 것을 고르시오.

1 There (is / are) four seasons in a year.
2 (Was / Were) there a key in your bag?
3 There (wasn't / weren't) many cookies on the plate.
4 (Is / Are) there comic books in the bookstore?
5 There (was / were) an event at the mall.
6 There (isn't / aren't) enough time.

season 몡 계절
plate 몡 접시
comic book 만화책
bookstore 몡 서점
event 몡 행사, 사건
enough 휑 충분한

B 다음 그림을 보고 빈칸에 알맞은 말을 <보기>에서 한 번씩만 골라 쓰시오.

1  2  3

glass 몡 (유리)잔
minute 몡 (시간 단위의) 분
people 몡 사람들
vase 몡 꽃병

| <보기> | there are | there was | there were |

1 _____ orange juice in the glass five minutes ago.
2 _____ four people in my family.
3 _____ two flowers in the vase yesterday.

C 우리말과 같도록 there와 괄호 안의 말을 활용하여 빈칸에 쓰시오.

1 도서관에 프린터 네 대가 있다. (four printers)
= _____ _____ _____ _____ in the library.

2 침대 위에 인형 한 개가 있니? (a doll)
= _____ _____ _____ _____ on the bed?

3 병 안에 콜라가 많지 않았다. (much coke)
= _____ _____ _____ in the bottle.

4 도로에 버스가 많지 않다. (many buses)
= _____ _____ _____ on the road.

library 몡 도서관
coke 몡 콜라

Chapter 03

be동사

Hackers Grammar Smart Starter

Writing Exercise

A 밑줄 친 부분이 어법상 맞으면 O를 쓰고, 틀리면 바르게 고쳐 쓰시오.

1 Judy and I <u>isn't</u> close. → _____

2 Busan <u>are</u> a big city in South Korea. → _____

3 There <u>are</u> seven cars in the parking lot. → _____

4 My father <u>were</u> at the theater yesterday. → _____

5 There <u>isn't</u> many carrots in the grocery store. → _____

6 <u>Was</u> James on the school bus 20 minutes ago? → _____

B 우리말과 같도록 괄호 안의 말과 be동사를 활용하여 문장을 완성하시오.

1 오늘은 월요일이 아니다. (it)

= _____ Monday today.

2 너의 지갑 안에 충분한 돈이 있었니? (there)

= _____ enough money in your wallet?

3 Jeffrey는 나쁜 소년이 아니었다. (Jeffrey)

= _____ a bad boy.

4 우리는 같은 고향에서 오지 않았다. (we)

= _____ from the same hometown.

5 나의 컴퓨터에는 많은 게임이 있었다. (there)

= _____ many games on my computer.

6 너의 친구들은 높은 곳을 무서워하니? (your friends)

= _____ afraid of high places?

7 Green 선생님은 나의 담임 선생님이시다. (Ms. Green)

= _____ my homeroom teacher.

C 우리말과 같도록 괄호 안의 말을 알맞게 배열하시오.

1 경기장에 많은 팬들이 있다. (many fans, are, there)

= _____ at the stadium.

2 그의 책은 유명하지 않았다. (famous, his book, not, was)

= _____ .

3 너는 이번 주말에 바쁘니? (busy, you, are)

= _____ this weekend?

4 뒷마당에 텐트가 있었니? (was, a tent, there)

= _____ in the backyard?

5 그것들은 Bill의 운동화가 아니었다. (Bill's sneakers, they, not, were)

= _____ .

D 다음 그림을 보고 be동사와 <보기>의 말을 활용하여 문장을 완성하시오.

Six Years Ago

Now

<보기>	short	a big TV	thin	long	a small TV	fat

1 Sharon's dogs _____ six years ago.

2 Sharon's dogs _____ now.

3 Sharon's hair _____ six years ago.

4 Sharon's hair _____ now.

5 There _____ in the living room six years ago.

6 There _____ in the living room now.

Chapter Test

[1-4] 다음 빈칸에 들어갈 알맞은 것을 고르시오.

1

We _____ on a soccer team.

① am ② is ③ are
④ was ⑤ be

2

There _____ juice in the glass.

① be ② is ③ are
④ am ⑤ were

3

_____ Mariah late for school yesterday?

① Am ② Is ③ Are
④ Was ⑤ Were

4

Jack and Eric _____ in Paris last week.

① am not ② isn't ③ aren't
④ wasn't ⑤ weren't

5 다음 중 밑줄 친 부분의 줄임말이 <u>잘못된</u> 것은?

① It <u>is not</u> sunny today. → isn't
② We <u>are not</u> in the library. → aren't
③ They <u>were not</u> upset. → weren't
④ My sister <u>was not</u> tall. → wasn't
⑤ I <u>am not</u> a dancer. → amn't

[6-7] 다음 중 밑줄 친 부분이 어법상 <u>어색한</u> 것을 고르시오.

6 ① The cats <u>are</u> on the sofa.
② She <u>were</u> with Jamie.
③ I <u>am</u> a member of the book club.
④ Mr. Wood <u>is</u> my English teacher.
⑤ That car <u>was</u> very expensive.

7 ① They <u>were</u> busy last weekend.
② Ms. Smith <u>is</u> not in the kitchen.
③ <u>Is</u> Susan at the hospital now?
④ I <u>was</u> at the airport yesterday.
⑤ Nate and I <u>are</u> classmates two years ago.

서술형

[8-10] be동사를 활용하여 문장을 완성하시오.

8

I was 12 years old last year. I _____ 13 years old now.

9

There _____ three oranges in the fridge an hour ago. There were five oranges an hour ago.

10

Fred and Natalie are middle school students. They _____ elementary school students.

11 다음 대화의 빈칸에 들어갈 말이 순서대로 짝지어진 것은?

> A: _____ there a wallet on the floor?
> B: No, there _____.

① Is – isn't
② Is – aren't
③ Are – is
④ Are – isn't
⑤ Are – aren't

12 다음 중 자연스럽지 않은 대화는?

① A: Was there a cookie in the jar?
　 B: No, there wasn't.
② A: Are you a nurse?
　 B: No, I'm not. I'm a doctor.
③ A: Were Hannah and Matt on the train?
　 B: Yes, they were.
④ A: Are you and William tired?
　 B: Yes, you are.
⑤ A: Is the weather good?
　 B: No, it isn't. It's rainy.

고난도

13 다음 중 밑줄 친 be동사의 의미가 나머지 넷과 다른 것은?

① My sister <u>is</u> in her room.
② I <u>am</u> at the history museum.
③ The girl <u>was</u> on the street.
④ These men <u>are</u> police officers.
⑤ Tom and Shawn <u>were</u> in the gym.

서술형

[14-15] 우리말과 같도록 괄호 안의 말을 알맞게 배열하시오.

14
> Sam은 지금 졸리지 않다. (sleepy, Sam, not, is)

= _____ now.

15
> 저 수학 문제들은 어려웠니? (those, difficult, were, math problems)

= _____ ?

서술형

[16-18] 우리말과 같도록 괄호 안의 말을 활용하여 문장을 완성하시오.

16
> 나의 가장 친한 친구는 Amy이다. (my best friend)

= _____ Amy.

17
> 냉장고 안에 사과가 있었다. (there, apples)

= _____ in the fridge.

18
> 어제는 춥지 않았다. (it, cold)

= _____ yesterday.

Chapter 03 be동사

Hackers Grammar Smart Starter

Word Review

Chapter 03에 나온 어휘 중 잘 외워지지 않는 것은 박스에 체크하여 복습하시오.

☐ busy	형 바쁜	☐ free	형 한가한, 자유의
☐ hungry	형 배고픈	☐ nervous	형 긴장한
☐ cook	명 요리사	☐ heavy	형 무거운
☐ doctor	명 의사	☐ sure	형 확신하는, 확실한
☐ handsome	형 멋진, 잘생긴	☐ elevator	명 엘리베이터
☐ pilot	명 조종사	☐ pond	명 연못
☐ firefighter	명 소방관	☐ season	명 계절
☐ honest	형 정직한	☐ hometown	명 고향
☐ cheap	형 (값이) 싼	☐ afraid of	~을 무서워하는
☐ lonely	형 외로운	☐ place	명 곳, 장소
☐ backpack	명 배낭	☐ stadium	명 경기장
☐ noisy	형 시끄러운	☐ wallet	명 지갑
☐ rude	형 무례한	☐ jar	명 병, 단지
☐ full	형 배가 부른	☐ museum	명 박물관
☐ ago	부 ~ 전에	☐ sleepy	형 졸리는, 졸음이 오는

Check-up

영어 어휘와 알맞은 우리말 뜻을 연결하시오.

1 lonely ・ ・ⓐ 병, 단지
2 jar ・ ・ⓑ 바쁜
3 season ・ ・ⓒ 외로운
4 nervous ・ ・ⓓ 긴장한
5 busy ・ ・ⓔ 계절

6 ago ・ ・ⓐ ~ 전에
7 backpack ・ ・ⓑ 졸리는, 졸음이 오는
8 pond ・ ・ⓒ 연못
9 sleepy ・ ・ⓓ ~을 무서워하는
10 afraid of ・ ・ⓔ 배낭

ⓓ01 ⓑ6 ⓒ8 ⓔ7 ⓐ9 ⓑ5 ⓓ4 ⓔ3 ⓐ2 ⓒ1 **정답**

Chapter

04

일반동사

일반동사는 주어의 동작이나 상태를 나타내는 동사로,
나타내는 시점과 주어에 따라 형태가 달라진다.

1 **일반동사**

주어의 동작이나 상태를 나타내는 동사이다.

go, eat, drink, speak, study, play, sleep, have, want, like, think 등

2 **일반동사 현재형의 쓰임**

일반동사의 현재형은 현재의 사실이나 반복되는 일을 나타낼 때 쓴다.

I **like** animals.
Emma **reads** books every day.

3 **일반동사 현재형의 형태**

❶ 주어가 1·2인칭이나 3인칭 복수인 경우 동사원형을 쓰고, 3인칭 단수인 경우 동사원형에 -(e)s를 붙인다.

1·2인칭이나 3인칭 복수 (I / We / You / They)	동사원형
3인칭 단수 (He / She / It)	동사원형 + -(e)s

We **live** in Busan.
He **goes** to bed at 10 P.M.

❷ 일반동사의 3인칭 단수 현재형 만드는 법

대부분의 동사	동사원형 + -s	eat – eat**s** sleep – sleep**s**	play – play**s** want – want**s**
-o, -s, -x, -ch, -sh로 끝나는 동사	동사원형 + -es	go – go**es** mix – mix**es**	miss – miss**es** watch – watch**es**
「자음 + y」로 끝나는 동사	y를 i로 바꾸고 + -es	cry – cr**ies** worry – worr**ies**	try – tr**ies** study – stud**ies**
불규칙하게 변하는 동사	have – **has**		

My brother **studies** English.
An ant **has** six legs.

Smart Check 다음 빈칸에 들어갈 알맞은 것을 고르시오.

1 They _____ a bottle of milk.
① drink ② drinks

2 Jenny _____ her hair in the morning.
① washs ② washes

Practice

Answers p.5

A 다음 동사의 3인칭 단수 현재형을 쓰시오.

1 look   –   _____

2 hurry   –   _____

3 finish   –   _____

4 learn   –   _____

5 make   –   _____

6 pass   –   _____

7 touch   –   _____

8 run   –   _____

9 fly   –   _____

10 stay   –   _____

11 have   –   _____

12 do   –   _____

hurry 동 서두르다
finish 동 끝내다
learn 동 배우다
pass 동 건네주다, 지나가다
touch 동 만지다
stay 동 머무르다

B 괄호 안의 동사를 현재형으로 바꿔 빈칸에 쓰시오.

1 Lucy _____ about me. (worry)

2 We _____ dinner at 7. (eat)

3 This water _____ from the lake. (come)

4 Mr. Davis _____ science at a high school. (teach)

dinner 명 저녁 (식사)
come from ~에서 나오다
lake 명 호수
high school 고등학교

C 다음 그림을 보고 <보기>의 동사를 활용하여 빈칸에 쓰시오. (단, 현재형으로 쓰시오.)

1    **2**    **3**

work 동 일하다
practice 동 연습하다
uncle 명 삼촌
cereal 명 시리얼

<보기>	work	practice	have

1 They _____ taekwondo in the afternoon.

2 My uncle _____ at a bakery.

3 Julie _____ cereal in the morning.

1 일반동사 현재형의 부정문

「주어 + do/does not + 동사원형」의 형태이다.

1·2인칭이나 3인칭 복수 (I / We / You / They)	do not[don't] + 동사원형
3인칭 단수 (He / She / It)	does not[doesn't] + 동사원형

I do not[don't] walk to school.
My brother does not[doesn't] need a bag.

2 일반동사 현재형의 의문문

「Do/Does + 주어 + 동사원형 ~?」의 형태이며, 긍정의 대답은 「Yes, 주어 + do/does.」, 부정의 대답은 「No, 주어 + don't/doesn't.」의 형태이다.

일반동사 현재형의 의문문				긍정의 대답	부정의 대답
1·2인칭이나 3인칭 복수	Do	I	동사원형 ~?	Yes, you do.	No, you don't.
		we		Yes, we/you do.	No, we/you don't.
		you		Yes, I/we do.	Yes, I/we don't.
		they		Yes, they do.	No, they don't.
3인칭 단수	Does	he		Yes, he does.	No, he doesn't.
		she		Yes, she does.	No, she doesn't.
		it		Yes, it does.	No, it doesn't.

A: **Do you get** up early?
B: **Yes, I do. / No, I don't.**

A: **Does Lisa drink** coffee?
B: **Yes, she does. / No, she doesn't.**

Smart Check   다음 빈칸에 들어갈 알맞은 것을 고르시오.

1 He _____ eat sweet food.

① don't   ② doesn't

2 _____ we have scissors?

① Do   ② Does

Practice

Answers p.5

A 괄호 안에서 알맞은 것을 고르시오.

1 Ellen (don't / doesn't) cook at home.

2 I (don't / doesn't) trust them.

3 Does he (know / knows) my phone number?

4 (Do / Does) Eric and Steve like strawberries?

5 My sister doesn't (sleep / sleeps) late.

cook 통 요리하다
trust 통 믿다
know 통 알다
phone number 전화 번호
strawberry 명 딸기
sleep late 늦잠을 자다

B 다음 문장을 부정문으로 바꿔 쓰시오.

1 We have vacation plans.

→ _____ vacation plans.

2 It rains every night.

→ _____ every night.

3 Clara watches horror movies.

→ _____ horror movies.

4 His parents exercise at the gym.

→ _____ at the gym.

5 Ms. Smith works at the hospital.

→ _____ at the hospital.

6 I take piano lessons.

→ _____ piano lessons.

vacation 명 방학
horror movie 공포 영화
exercise 통 운동하다
hospital 명 병원
take a lesson 수업을 받다

C 괄호 안의 동사를 활용하여 대화를 완성하시오. (단, 현재형으로 쓰시오.)

1 A: _____ you _____ my help? (need)
B: No, I _____.

2 A: _____ they _____ Korean? (speak)
B: No, they _____.

3 A: _____ this dress _____ pretty? (look)
B: Yes, it _____.

4 A: _____ Donald _____ a bicycle at the park? (ride)
B: No, he _____.

5 A: _____ you and your friends _____ some snacks? (want)
B: Yes, we _____.

help 명 도움; 통 돕다
need 통 필요하다
speak 통 말하다
look 통 ~하게 보이다
ride 통 타다
snack 명 간식

UNIT 03 | 일반동사의 과거형

1 일반동사 과거형의 쓰임

일반동사의 과거형은 과거의 동작이나 상태를 나타낼 때 쓴다.

I **finished** my homework.
Kelly **learned** tennis last year.
↳ 과거형은 yesterday, last week, two months ago 등의 과거를 나타내는 표현과 주로 함께 쓰인다.

2 일반동사 과거형의 형태

❶ 일반동사의 과거형은 대부분 동사원형에 -(e)d를 붙여 만든다.

대부분의 동사	동사원형 + -ed	talk – talk**ed** work – work**ed**	clean – clean**ed** stay – stay**ed**
-e로 끝나는 동사	동사원형 + -d	love – lov**ed** save – sav**ed**	live – liv**ed** dance – danc**ed**
「자음 + y」로 끝나는 동사	y를 i로 바꾸고 + -ed	study – stud**ied** hurry – hurr**ied**	worry – worr**ied** try – tr**ied**
「단모음 + 단자음」으로 끝나는 동사	마지막 자음을 한 번 더 쓰고 + -ed	stop – stop**ped** jog – jog**ged**	plan – plan**ned** shop – shop**ped**

He **worked** last weekend.
George and I **jogged** together.

❷ 일부 일반동사의 과거형은 불규칙하게 변한다.

현재형과 과거형이 같은 동사	put – **put**	cut – **cut**	hit – **hit**	read – **read**
현재형과 과거형이 다른 동사	run – **ran** sing – **sang** come – **came** find – **found** tell – **told** sleep – **slept**	get – **got** swim – **swam** drink – **drank** have – **had** see – **saw** go – **went**	win – **won** wake – **woke** give – **gave** make – **made** eat – **ate** buy – **bought**	sit – **sat** meet – **met** write – **wrote** hear – **heard** do – **did** teach – **taught**

I **put** the vase on the table.
Hannah **heard** a strange sound last night.

Smart Check 다음 빈칸에 들어갈 알맞은 것을 고르시오.

1 We _____ to Seoul two weeks ago.
  ① move   ② moved

2 My father _____ history at a school.
  ① taught   ② teached

Practice

Answers p.6

A 다음 동사의 과거형을 쓰시오.

1 need – _____

2 like – _____

3 go – _____

4 try – _____

5 cut – _____

6 use – _____

7 walk – _____

8 plan – _____

9 give – _____

10 eat – _____

11 watch – _____

12 buy – _____

use 동 사용하다
walk 동 걷다
watch 동 보다
buy 동 사다

B 괄호 안의 동사를 과거형으로 바꿔 빈칸에 쓰시오.

1 We _____ in the hallway. (run)

2 The baseball player _____ the ball. (hit)

3 Jeffrey _____ English yesterday. (study)

4 I _____ my neighbor at the café. (meet)

5 The snow _____ an hour ago. (stop)

hallway 명 복도
baseball player 야구 선수
neighbor 명 이웃
snow 명 눈

C 다음 그림을 보고 <보기>의 동사를 활용하여 빈칸에 쓰시오. (단, 과거형으로 쓰시오.)

1  **2**  **3**

gold medal 금메달

| <보기> | start | see | win |

1 Nicole _____ a ghost in her dreams.

2 They _____ the gold medal last year.

3 Summer vacation _____ three days ago.

Chapter 04

일반동사

Hackers Grammar Smart Starter

UNIT 04 | 일반동사 과거형의 부정문과 의문문

1 ## 일반동사 과거형의 부정문

「주어 + did not[didn't] + 동사원형」의 형태이다.

1·2인칭이나 3인칭 복수 (I / We / You / They)	did not[didn't] + 동사원형
3인칭 단수 (He / She / It)	

I did not[didn't] drink your juice.
She did not[didn't] use the computer.
Carl's mom did not[didn't] cook spaghetti.

---

2 ## 일반동사 과거형의 의문문

「Did + 주어 + 동사원형 ~?」의 형태이며, 긍정의 대답은 「Yes, 주어 + did.」, 부정의 대답은 「No, 주어 + didn't.」의 형태이다.

주어	일반동사 과거형의 의문문	긍정의 대답	부정의 대답
1·2인칭이나 3인칭 복수 (I / We / You / They)	Did + 주어 + 동사원형 ~?	Yes, 주어 + did.	No, 주어 + didn't.
3인칭 단수 (He / She / It)			

A: **Did you see** the bird?
B: **Yes, I did. / No, I didn't.**

A: **Did the students make** trouble?
B: **Yes, they did. / No, they didn't.**

A: **Did Roy plant** the trees?
B: **Yes, he did. / No, he didn't.**

Smart Check 다음 빈칸에 들어갈 알맞은 것을 고르시오.

1 They didn't _____ a car.
① bought   ② buy

2 _____ she listen to music yesterday?
① Does   ② Did

Practice

A 괄호 안에서 알맞은 것을 고르시오.

1 He and I (don't / didn't) talk an hour ago.

2 Kelly didn't (stay / stayed) at the hotel.

3 (Do / Did) you read a book last night?

4 Brian (doesn't / didn't) feel good yesterday.

5 Did she (borrow / borrowed) an umbrella?

talk 통 이야기하다
feel 통 ~하게 느끼다
borrow 통 빌리다
umbrella 명 우산

B 다음 문장을 부정문으로 바꿔 쓰시오.

1 He failed the test yesterday.

→ _____ the test yesterday.

2 Angela made a mistake.

→ _____ a mistake.

3 I got a cold last winter.

→ _____ a cold last winter.

4 The woman found the key.

→ _____ the key.

5 Ms. Green cut her hair last month.

→ _____ her hair last month.

fail 통 떨어지다, 실패하다
make a mistake 실수하다
get a cold 감기에 걸리다
winter 명 겨울

C 괄호 안의 동사를 활용하여 대화를 완성하시오.

1 A: _____ Emily _____ her friends three days ago? (invite)

B: Yes, she _____.

2 A: _____ you _____ a present to Tom yesterday? (give)

B: No, I _____.

3 A: _____ they _____ to the concert last Friday? (go)

B: Yes, they _____.

4 A: _____ you and Dave _____ there a week ago? (visit)

B: No, we _____.

5 A: _____ Dad _____ at the airport last night? (arrive)

B: Yes, he _____.

invite 통 초대하다
present 명 선물
visit 통 방문하다
arrive 통 도착하다

Writing Exercise

A 우리말과 같도록 괄호 안의 동사를 활용하여 문장을 완성하시오.

1 Tony는 그의 친구들과 수다를 떨었다. (chat)

= _____ with his friends.

2 나는 커피숍에서 공부하지 않는다. (study)

= _____ at coffee shops.

3 그녀는 작년에 스페인어를 배웠니? (learn)

= _____ Spanish last year?

4 그의 삼촌은 여름마다 수영장에 가신다. (go)

= _____ to the swimming pool every summer.

5 Janet은 빨간 장미를 좋아하니? (like)

= _____ red roses?

6 그들은 차 안에 그 상자를 두지 않았다. (put)

= _____ the box in the car.

B 우리말과 같도록 괄호 안의 말을 알맞게 배열하시오.

1 나는 어제 그 나쁜 소식을 들었다. (heard, I, the bad news)

= _____ yesterday.

2 나의 개가 어젯밤에 큰 소리로 짖었니? (my dog, did, bark)

= _____ loudly last night?

3 너는 오늘 영어 수업이 있니? (have, you, an English class, do)

= _____ today?

4 Terry는 나에게 편지를 쓰지 않았다. (not, Terry, write, did, a letter)

= _____ to me.

5 Megan과 나는 일요일마다 산을 오른다. (climb, Megan and I, mountains)

= _____ on Sundays.

6 그 학생은 그 선생님의 이름을 기억하지 못한다. (remember, the student, not, does)

= _____ the teacher's name.

C 다음은 Kate가 자신의 가족을 소개하는 글이다. 괄호 안의 동사를 활용하여 빈칸에 쓰시오.

Hello, everyone. Let me introduce my family.

My family ⓐ _____ (move) to Korea two years ago.

And we ⓑ _____ (live) in Seoul now.

My father ⓒ _____ (work) at a middle school now.

He ⓓ _____ (teach) high school students last year.

My mother is a cook. She ⓔ _____ (make) delicious food every day.

My sister is a dancer. She always ⓕ _____ (try) her best.

So, she ⓖ _____ (pass) an audition last week.

D 다음 그림을 보고 괄호 안의 말을 활용하여 대화를 완성하시오.

1  **2**  **3**  **4**

1 *A*: _____ a bus to school? (Martha, take)

　　B: No, she doesn't.

2 *A*: _____ badminton yesterday? (Ken and Ian, play)

　　B: No, they didn't.

3 *A*: _____ chopsticks? (you, use)

　　B: Yes, I do.

4 *A*: _____ on the sofa an hour ago? (the puppies, sleep)

　　B: No, they didn't.

1 다음 중 동사의 3인칭 단수 현재형이 <u>잘못된</u> 것은?

① fix – fixes   ② need – needs

③ worry – worries   ④ have – has

⑤ wash – washs

2 다음 중 동사의 과거형이 <u>잘못된</u> 것은?

① drop – dropped   ② sing – sang

③ hurry – hurried   ④ play – plaied

⑤ practice – practiced

[3-5] 다음 빈칸에 들어갈 알맞은 것을 고르시오.

3

_____ works at the post office.

① I   ② You

③ The women   ④ We

⑤ Mr. Scott

4

We _____ a mountain every weekend.

① climb   ② climbs

③ doesn't climbs   ④ don't climbs

⑤ doesn't climb

5

The students _____ to the museum last month.

① go   ② goes

③ don't go   ④ didn't go

⑤ didn't went

서술형

[6-7] 다음 빈칸에 알맞은 말을 넣어 질문에 대한 대답을 완성하시오.

6

A: Do they know each other?

B: Yes, _____ _____.

7

A: Did the accident happen last night?

B: No, _____ _____.

[8-9] 다음 중 밑줄 친 부분이 어법상 <u>어색한</u> 것을 고르시오.

8 ① Eric <u>rides</u> his bike every day.

② They <u>planted</u> trees yesterday.

③ Amy <u>buys</u> a lamp last weekend.

④ My mom <u>loves</u> my brother and me.

⑤ I <u>watch</u> television in the evening.

9 ① Did I <u>leave</u> the key at home?

② Does Kathy and Bill <u>like</u> pizza?

③ George <u>didn't do</u> his homework.

④ This café <u>doesn't open</u> on Tuesday.

⑤ Do they <u>remember</u> my address?

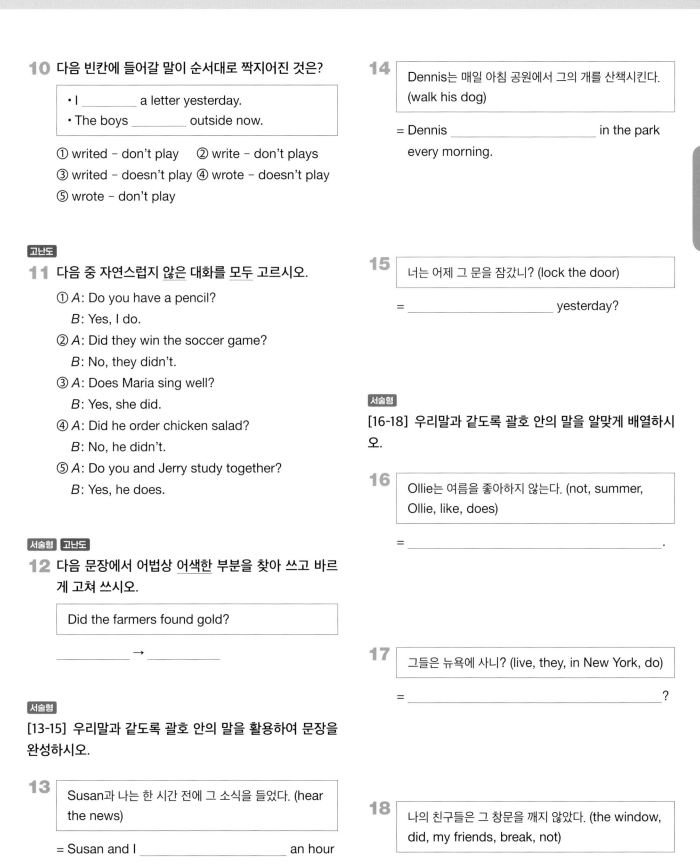

10 다음 빈칸에 들어갈 말이 순서대로 짝지어진 것은?

- I _____ a letter yesterday.
- The boys _____ outside now.

① writed – don't play   ② write – don't plays

③ writed – doesn't play ④ wrote – doesn't play

⑤ wrote – don't play

`고난도`

11 다음 중 자연스럽지 않은 대화를 모두 고르시오.

① A: Do you have a pencil?
   B: Yes, I do.

② A: Did they win the soccer game?
   B: No, they didn't.

③ A: Does Maria sing well?
   B: Yes, she did.

④ A: Did he order chicken salad?
   B: No, he didn't.

⑤ A: Do you and Jerry study together?
   B: Yes, he does.

`서술형` `고난도`

12 다음 문장에서 어법상 어색한 부분을 찾아 쓰고 바르게 고쳐 쓰시오.

Did the farmers found gold?

_____ → _____

`서술형`

[13-15] 우리말과 같도록 괄호 안의 말을 활용하여 문장을 완성하시오.

13

Susan과 나는 한 시간 전에 그 소식을 들었다. (hear the news)

= Susan and I _____ an hour ago.

14

Dennis는 매일 아침 공원에서 그의 개를 산책시킨다. (walk his dog)

= Dennis _____ in the park every morning.

15

너는 어제 그 문을 잠갔니? (lock the door)

= _____ yesterday?

`서술형`

[16-18] 우리말과 같도록 괄호 안의 말을 알맞게 배열하시오.

16

Ollie는 여름을 좋아하지 않는다. (not, summer, Ollie, like, does)

= _____ .

17

그들은 뉴욕에 사니? (live, they, in New York, do)

= _____ ?

18

나의 친구들은 그 창문을 깨지 않았다. (the window, did, my friends, break, not)

= _____ .

Word Review

Chapter 04에 나온 어휘 중 잘 외워지지 않는 것은 박스에 체크하여 복습하시오.

□ speak	동 말하다	□ try	동 시도하다
□ hurry	동 서두르다	□ hear	동 듣다
□ finish	동 끝내다, 끝나다	□ strange	형 이상한
□ learn	동 배우다	□ history	명 역사
□ pass	동 건네주다, 지나가다	□ use	동 사용하다
□ stay	동 머무르다	□ hallway	명 복도
□ worry about	~에 대해 걱정하다	□ ghost	명 유령
□ lake	명 호수	□ plant	동 심다
□ practice	동 연습하다	□ fail	동 떨어지다, 실패하다
□ afternoon	명 오후	□ mistake	명 실수
□ early	부 일찍; 형 이른	□ put	동 두다, 놓다
□ trust	동 믿다	□ climb	동 오르다
□ know	동 알다	□ remember	동 기억하다
□ vacation	명 방학	□ introduce	동 소개하다
□ ride	동 타다	□ drop	동 떨어뜨리다

Check-up

영어 어휘와 알맞은 우리말 뜻을 연결하시오.

1 try · · ⓐ 호수
2 drop · · ⓑ 떨어뜨리다
3 lake · · ⓒ 배우다
4 learn · · ⓓ 시도하다
5 hear · · ⓔ 듣다

6 climb · · ⓐ 이상한
7 pass · · ⓑ 건네주다, 지나가다
8 stay · · ⓒ ~에 대해 걱정하다
9 worry about · · ⓓ 오르다
10 strange · · ⓔ 머무르다

정답 1ⓓ 2ⓑ 3ⓐ 4ⓒ 5ⓔ 6ⓓ 7ⓑ 8ⓔ 9ⓒ 10ⓐ

Chapter

05

형용사와 부사

형용사는 명사나 대명사를 꾸미거나 주어를 보충 설명한다.
부사는 동사, 형용사, 다른 부사, 문장 전체를 꾸민다.

UNIT 01 | 형용사

1 형용사의 쓰임

❶ 주로 명사 앞에서 명사를 꾸민다.

Linda is a **smart** *girl*.
He has **new** *pencils*.

> **TIP** -thing으로 끝나는 대명사를 꾸밀 때는 형용사가 대명사 뒤에 온다.
> I want *something* **sweet**.

❷ 동사 뒤에서 주어를 보충 설명한다.

My father is **gentle**.
The bags are **heavy**.

> **TIP** 형용사와 함께 자주 쓰이는 동사: **be, become, look, sound, smell, taste, feel** 등
> She *looks* **angry**.
> This soup *smells* **delicious**.

2 many, much

❶ many는 '(수가) 많은'이라는 의미로, 셀 수 있는 명사의 복수형 앞에 쓴다.

There are **many** *children* in the park.

❷ much는 '(양이) 많은'이라는 의미로, 셀 수 없는 명사 앞에 쓴다.

I don't need **much** *butter*.

3 some, any

'약간의, 조금의, 몇몇의'라는 의미로, 셀 수 있는 명사의 복수형과 셀 수 없는 명사 앞에 모두 쓸 수 있다.

❶ some은 주로 긍정문과 권유를 나타내는 의문문에 쓴다.

She bought **some** *oranges*.
Do you want **some** *water*?

❷ any는 주로 부정문과 의문문에 쓴다.

He doesn't have **any** *plans*.
Did they find **any** *food*?

Smart Check   다음 빈칸에 들어갈 알맞은 것을 고르시오.

1 They are _____.

① dogs lovely   ② lovely dogs

2 Charles baked _____ cookies.

① many   ② much

영어 실력을 높여주는 다양한 학습 자료 제공 HackersBook.com

Practice

Answers p.7

A 다음 그림을 보고 빈칸에 알맞은 형용사를 <보기>에서 한 번씩만 골라 쓰시오.

> <보기>   hot   cloudy   curly   tired   yellow   round

cloudy 형 흐린, 구름이 잔뜩 낀
curly 형 곱슬곱슬한
tired 형 피곤한
round 형 둥근
weather 명 날씨

1

My sister's dress is
_____.

2

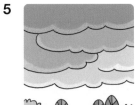

The woman looks
_____.

3

There is _____
tea in the cup.

4

It's a _____
table.

5

The weather is
_____.

6

Matthew has
_____ hair.

B 괄호 안에서 알맞은 것을 고르시오.

1 There is a (tall tree / tree tall).

2 That pasta tastes (salt / salty).

3 He didn't get (many / much) sleep.

4 They saw (scary something / something scary) yesterday.

sleep 명 잠; 동 자다
scary 형 무서운

C 우리말과 같도록 빈칸에 알맞은 형용사를 <보기>에서 골라 쓰시오.

> <보기>   many   much   some   any

advice 명 조언
take care of ~을 돌보다
town 명 마을
save 동 절약하다, 구하다

1 나는 너에게서 몇 가지 조언을 원한다.
= I want _____ advice from you.

2 그녀는 지난주에 많은 개들을 돌봤다.
= She took care of _____ dogs last week.

3 그 마을에는 카페가 전혀 없다.
= There aren't _____ cafés in the town.

4 그 학생들은 많은 시간을 절약했다.
= The students saved _____ time.

UNIT 02 | 부사

1 부사의 쓰임

동사, 형용사, 다른 부사, 문장 전체를 꾸민다.

I *study* **hard**. <동사 수식>

Your skirt is **so** *pretty*. <형용사 수식>

Betty swims **very** *well*. <다른 부사 수식>

Finally, *he found his wallet*. <문장 전체 수식>

2 부사의 형태

부사는 대부분 형용사에 -ly를 붙여 만든다.

대부분의 형용사	형용사 + -ly	slow – slow**ly**	real – real**ly**
「자음 + y」로 끝나는 형용사	y를 i로 바꾸고 + -ly	happy – happ**ily**	easy – eas**ily**
-le로 끝나는 형용사	e를 없애고 + -y	simple – simpl**y**	gentle – gentl**y**
불규칙하게 변하는 부사	good – **well**		
형용사와 형태가 같은 부사	late(늦은) – **late**(늦게) hard(어려운, 단단한) – **hard**(열심히) fast(빠른) – **fast**(빠르게)	early(이른) – **early**(일찍) high(높은) – **high**(높게, 높이)	

TIP friendly(친절한), lovely(사랑스러운), lonely(외로운), weekly(주간의)는 -ly로 끝나지만 부사가 아닌 형용사이다.
They are really **friendly**.

3 빈도부사

❶ 어떤 일이 얼마나 자주 발생하는지를 나타내는 부사이다.

100%					0%
always	usually	often	sometimes	seldom	never
(항상)	(보통, 대개)	(종종, 자주)	(때때로, 가끔)	(거의 ~않다)	(결코 ~않다)

I **usually** have dinner at 7 P.M.

They **sometimes** do volunteer work.

❷ be동사나 조동사 뒤 또는 일반동사 앞에 온다.

Your room *is* **always** clean.

He **never** *watches* TV.

다음 문장의 밑줄 친 부사가 수식하는 부분에 동그라미를 치시오.

1 Emily speaks <u>loudly</u>.

2 These pants are <u>so</u> small.

3 <u>Finally</u>, I finished my homework.

4 He answered <u>very</u> quickly.

Practice

Answers p.7

A 다음 형용사를 부사로 바꿔 쓰시오.

1 soft   – _____   **6** early   – _____

2 heavy   – _____   **7** quiet   – _____

3 fast   – _____   **8** clear   – _____

4 possible   – _____   **9** noisy   – _____

5 wise   – _____   **10** horrible   – _____

possible 형 가능한
wise 형 지혜로운
clear 형 분명한
noisy 형 시끄러운
horrible 형 끔찍한

B 괄호 안에서 알맞은 것을 고르시오.

1 (Sad / Sadly), he broke his arm.

2 She (is often / often is) sick in winter.

3 Peter plays the guitar (good / well).

4 These shoes fit me (perfect / perfectly).

5 They (sometimes exercise / exercise sometimes) together.

arm 명 팔
fit 동 맞다, 적합하다
exercise 동 운동하다
together 부 함께

C 다음 표를 보고 빈칸에 알맞은 빈도부사를 <보기>에서 골라 쓰시오.

	Mon	Tue	Wed	Thu	Fri
David	🚇	🚌	🚇	🚌	🚇
Lisa	🚶	🚌	🚌	🚌	🚌
Paul	🚶	🚶	🚶	🚶	🚶

take 동 (교통수단을) 타다
subway 명 지하철
walk 동 걷다

<보기>	always	usually	often	seldom	never

1 David _____ takes the subway to school.

2 Lisa _____ walks to school.

3 Lisa _____ takes the bus to school.

4 Paul _____ takes the subway to school.

5 Paul _____ walks to school.

Chapter 05

형용사와 부사

Hackers Grammar Smart Starter

Writing Exercise

A 우리말과 같도록 괄호 안의 말을 활용하여 빈칸에 쓰시오.

1 미술관 안에 많은 방문객들이 있었다. (visitors)

= There were _____ _____ in the gallery.

2 그들은 버스에서 큰 소리로 말했다. (loud)

= They talked _____ on the bus.

3 Nick은 때때로 점심 식사 후에 낮잠을 잔다. (take)

= Nick _____ _____ a nap after lunch.

4 그녀는 오늘 숙제가 전혀 없다. (homework)

= She doesn't have _____ _____ today.

5 우리는 춤 대회를 위해 열심히 연습했다. (hard)

= We practiced _____ for the dance contest.

6 나는 지난겨울에 많은 눈을 봤다. (snow)

= I saw _____ _____ last winter.

B 우리말과 같도록 괄호 안의 말을 알맞게 배열하시오.

1 Thomas는 오늘 잘생겨 보인다. (handsome, looks)

= Thomas _____ today.

2 그는 그의 딸에게 많은 사랑을 준다. (love, much, gives)

= He _____ to his daughter.

3 Ashley는 지금 아주 배고프다. (is, hungry, really)

= Ashley _____ now.

4 나는 저녁 식사로 매운 무언가를 원했다. (wanted, spicy, something)

= I _____ for dinner.

5 그들은 금요일마다 종종 바쁘다. (busy, often, are)

= They _____ on Fridays.

6 나의 어머니는 약간의 초콜릿 쿠키를 구우셨다. (baked, chocolate cookies, some)

= My mother _____.

C 다음 그림을 보고 <보기>의 말을 한 번씩만 활용하여 빈칸에 쓰시오.

1    2    3    4

<보기>	high	beautiful	cold	bright

1 There are _____ stars in the sky.

2 The ballerina performed _____.

3 Maria needs something _____.

4 Ken jumped _____ on a trampoline.

D 다음은 Olivia가 일주일 동안 하는 것과 하지 않는 것을 나타낸 표이다. <보기>의 빈도부사를 활용하여 문장을 완성하시오. (단, 현재형으로 쓰시오.)

	Sun	Mon	Tue	Wed	Thu	Fri	Sat
1 play tennis		V		V		V	V
2 eat breakfast	V	V	V	V	V	V	V
3 be late for school							
4 read a book			V				
5 take a piano lesson			V	V			

<보기>	always	often	sometimes	seldom	never

1 Olivia _____.

2 Olivia _____.

3 Olivia _____.

4 Olivia _____.

5 Olivia _____.

Chapter Test

[1-3] 다음 빈칸에 들어갈 말로 <u>어색한</u> 것을 고르시오.

1

> Emperor penguins are _____.

① strong   ② heavy   ③ slowly
④ tall   ⑤ cute

2

> Michelle is a _____ student.

① smart   ② new   ③ popular
④ lovely   ⑤ quietly

3

> Mr. Brown talked to the customer _____.

① friendly   ② gently   ③ softly
④ quickly   ⑤ kindly

[4-5] 다음 빈칸에 들어갈 말이 순서대로 짝지어진 것을 고르시오.

4

> • I bought _____ science books.
> • Are there _____ onions in the fridge?

① some – some   ② any – much
③ some – much   ④ any – any
⑤ some – any

5

> • Did you put _____ salt in the soup?
> • Charlie doesn't ask _____ questions in class.

① many – many   ② many – much
③ much – some   ④ much – many
⑤ much – much

6 밑줄 친 부분의 쓰임이 나머지 넷과 <u>다른</u> 것은?

① The airplane flies <u>really</u> high.
② They came home <u>early</u>.
③ <u>Sadly</u>, our team lost the final game.
④ I'm sometimes <u>lonely</u>.
⑤ My brother was <u>very</u> sleepy.

[7-8] 다음 중 괄호 안의 말이 들어갈 가장 알맞은 위치를 고르시오.

7

> I ① have ② a piece of ③ bread ④ for ⑤ breakfast. (always)

8

> My ① parents ② are ③ busy ④ in ⑤ the weekdays. (usually)

[9-10] 다음 중 밑줄 친 부분이 어법상 어색한 것을 고르시오.

9　① He needs <u>some</u> help with his homework.
　② Do you want <u>some</u> more rice?
　③ I don't have <u>any</u> red pens.
　④ There isn't <u>some</u> sugar in the bottle.
　⑤ Did Jenny receive <u>any</u> letters today?

10　① It rained <u>heavily</u> last summer.
　② The pizza smells <u>greatly</u>.
　③ Nate moved the boxes <u>carefully</u>.
　④ This bracelet is my <u>lucky</u> item.
　⑤ That is a <u>good</u> idea.

서술형 고난도

11 다음 두 문장의 의미가 같도록 빈칸에 알맞은 말을 쓰시오.

> Sarah was late for school.
> → Sarah came to school _____.

서술형 고난도

[12-15] 다음 문장에서 어법상 어색한 부분을 찾아 쓰고 바르게 고쳐 쓰시오.

12
> I spend too many money on snacks.

_____ → _____

13
> He took any medicine an hour ago.

_____ → _____

14
> Zebras run so fastly.

_____ → _____

15
> The English test was really easily.

_____ → _____

서술형 고난도

16 우리말과 같도록 괄호 안의 말을 알맞게 배열하시오.

> Miranda는 그녀의 생일을 위해 특별한 무언가를 원했다. (special, wanted, Miranda, something)

= _____ for her birthday.

Chapter 05

형용사와 부사

Hackers Grammar Smart Starter

Word Review

Chapter 05에 나온 어휘 중 잘 외워지지 않는 것은 박스에 체크하여 복습하시오.

□ gentle	형 온화한	□ possible	형 가능한
□ lovely	형 사랑스러운	□ wise	형 지혜로운
□ curly	형 곱슬곱슬한	□ clear	형 분명한
□ round	형 둥근	□ noisy	형 시끄러운
□ salty	형 짠, 짭짤한	□ horrible	형 끔찍한
□ scary	형 무서운	□ fit	동 맞다, 적합하다
□ advice	명 조언	□ perfectly	부 완벽하게
□ take care of	~을 돌보다	□ subway	명 지하철
□ town	명 마을	□ visitor	명 방문객
□ hard	부 열심히; 형 단단한	□ take a nap	낮잠을 자다
□ volunteer work	자원봉사	□ really	부 아주, 진짜로
□ clean	형 깨끗한	□ perform	동 공연하다, 행하다
□ loudly	부 큰 소리로, 시끄럽게	□ quietly	부 조용히
□ quickly	부 빨리, 곧	□ onion	명 양파
□ heavy	형 무거운, 심한	□ medicine	명 약

Check-up

영어 어휘와 알맞은 우리말 뜻을 연결하시오.

1	round	·	· ⓐ 둥근	6	curly	·	· ⓐ 조언
2	possible	·	· ⓑ ~을 돌보다	7	heavy	·	· ⓑ 곱슬곱슬한
3	fit	·	· ⓒ 지혜로운	8	advice	·	· ⓒ 공연하다, 행하다
4	wise	·	· ⓓ 가능한	9	clear	·	· ⓓ 분명한
5	take care of	·	· ⓔ 맞다, 적합하다	10	perform	·	· ⓔ 무거운, 심한

정답 1 ⓐ 2 ⓓ 3 ⓔ 4 ⓒ 5 ⓑ 6 ⓑ 7 ⓔ 8 ⓐ 9 ⓓ 10 ⓒ

Chapter

06

현재진행시제와
미래시제

시제는 동사의 형태를 바꿔 행동이나 사건이 발생한 시점을 표현하는 것이다.
현재진행시제는 지금 진행되고 있는 동작을 나타내고,
미래시제는 앞으로 일어날 일을 나타낸다.

UNIT 01 | 현재진행시제

1 현재진행시제의 쓰임

현재진행시제는 지금 진행되고 있는 동작을 나타내며, '~하고 있다, ~하는 중이다'의 의미이다.

He **is drinking** water now.

2 현재진행시제의 형태

❶ 「be동사의 현재형(am/are/is) + V-ing」의 형태이며, 이때 be동사는 주어의 인칭과 수에 따라 형태가 달라진다.

I **am studying**.
We **are going** to school.
Alan **is drawing** a picture.

❷ 동사의 V-ing형 만드는 법

대부분의 동사	동사원형 + -ing	do – do**ing**	play – play**ing**
「자음 + e」로 끝나는 동사	e를 빼고 + -ing	come – com**ing**	make – mak**ing**
-ie로 끝나는 동사	ie를 y로 바꾸고 + -ing	lie – **lying**	tie – **tying**
「단모음 + 단자음」으로 끝나는 동사	마지막 자음을 한 번 더 쓰고 + -ing	cut – cut**ting** sit – sit**ting**	run – run**ning** put – put**ting**

3 현재진행시제의 부정문과 의문문

❶ 현재진행시제의 부정문은 「주어 + be동사의 현재형 + not + V-ing」의 형태이다.

They're not lying on the floor.

❷ 현재진행시제의 의문문은 「be동사의 현재형 + 주어 + V-ing ~?」의 형태이며, 긍정의 대답은 「Yes, 주어 + be동사의 현재형.」, 부정의 대답은 「No, 주어 + be동사의 현재형 + not.」의 형태이다.

A: **Are you talking** to Judy?
B: **Yes, I am. / No, I'm not.**

Smart Check 다음 빈칸에 들어갈 알맞은 것을 고르시오.

1 My mom is _____ a magazine.
  ① reads ② reading

2 Are you _____ for your friend?
  ① wait ② waiting

3 I _____ listening to music.
  ① am not ② not am

Practice

Answers p.8

A 다음 동사의 V-ing형을 쓰시오.

1 live   – _____
2 tell   – _____
3 give   – _____
4 cut   – _____

5 stop   – _____
6 look   – _____
7 die   – _____
8 cry   – _____

live 동 살다
tell 동 말하다
give 동 주다
die 동 죽다
cry 동 울다

B 괄호 안의 말을 활용하여 현재진행시제 문장을 완성하시오.

1 I _____ the cello. (play)

2 The doctors _____ white coats. (wear)

3 The man _____ a horse. (not, ride)

4 They _____ in the park. (not, jog)

cello 명 첼로
wear 동 입다
ride 동 타다
jog 동 조깅하다

C 다음 그림을 보고 <보기>의 동사를 활용하여 대화를 완성하시오. (단, 현재진행시제로 쓰시오.)

watch 동 보다
living room 거실

| <보기> | watch | run | speak |

1 A: Is Eric washing the dishes?
    B: No, he isn't. He _____ _____ on the phone.

2 A: _____ Lucy and Fred _____ TV?
    B: Yes, they are.

3 A: Is the cat sleeping?
    B: No, it isn't. It _____ _____ in the living room.

UNIT 02 | 미래시제

1 미래시제의 쓰임과 형태

❶ 미래시제는 앞으로 일어날 일을 나타내며, '~할 것이다'의 의미이다. 미래시제는 「will + 동사원형」이나 「be going to + 동사원형」의 형태이다.

I **will meet** Bobby tomorrow.
She **is going to buy** a new bicycle.
     ↳ be going to의 be는 주어의 인칭과 수에 따라 형태가 달라진다.

❷ 미래시제는 tomorrow, next week, next month, soon 등의 미래를 나타내는 표현과 주로 함께 쓰인다.

It **will be** sunny *next week*.
They**'re going to leave** *soon*.

2 will이 있는 미래시제의 부정문과 의문문

부정문	의문문
주어 + will + not + 동사원형 ↳ won't	Will + 주어 + 동사원형 ~? – Yes, 주어 + will. / No, 주어 + won't.

My sister will not[won't] call me.

A: **Will you take** the bus?
B: **Yes, I will. / No, I won't.**

3 be going to가 있는 미래시제의 부정문과 의문문

부정문	의문문
주어 + be동사 + not + going to + 동사원형	be동사 + 주어 + going to + 동사원형 ~? – Yes, 주어 + be동사. / No, 주어 + be동사 + not.

Martin isn't going to go to the beach.

A: **Are we going to watch** this movie?
B: **Yes, we are. / No, we aren't.**

Smart Check 다음 빈칸에 들어갈 알맞은 것을 고르시오.

1 Kelly will _____ a hamburger.
  ① eat   ② eating

2 Will he _____ a picture?
  ① takes   ② take

3 I'm not going _____ a skirt.
  ① wear   ② to wear

Practice

Answers p.8

A   괄호 안에서 알맞은 것을 고르시오.

1 She will (pass / passes) the exam.

2 Mr. Adams is (take / going to take) a nap.

3 Sarah (willn't / won't) learn a musical instrument.

4 He is not going to (use / using) the glue.

5 (Is / Will) she going to make sandwiches?

6 Chris and I are going (come / to come) back soon.

7 Will (pack they / they pack) their bags tomorrow?

pass 동 합격하다, 지나가다
take a nap 낮잠을 자다
musical instrument 악기
glue 명 접착제, 풀
come back 돌아오다
pack 동 (짐 등을) 싸다

B   다음 그림을 보고 will과 <보기>의 동사를 활용하여 빈칸에 쓰시오.

1

2 The Test Schedule
• Math Test 10:00 ~10:50
• English Test 11:00 ~11:50

3

visit 동 방문하다
paint 동 페인트를 칠하다
museum 명 박물관
math 명 수학
wall 명 벽, 담

| <보기> | start | visit | paint |

1 Brian _____ _____ the museum next week.

2 The math test _____ _____ at 11 o'clock.

3 The woman _____ _____ the wall.

C   다음 문장을 be going to를 활용하여 바꿔 쓰시오.

1 I will tell you the truth.

→ _____ you the truth.

2 Will it rain tomorrow?

→ _____ tomorrow?

3 The field trip will be fun.

→ _____ fun.

4 We will not read the book again.

→ _____ the book again.

truth 명 사실
rain 동 비가 오다
field trip 현장 학습
fun 형 재미있는
again 부 또, 다시

Writing Exercise

A 우리말과 같도록 괄호 안의 동사를 활용하여 빈칸에 쓰시오.

1 그는 약속을 지키지 않을 것이다. (keep)

= He _____ _____ his promise.

2 나는 핫도그를 주문할 것이다. (order)

= I _____ _____ _____ _____ a hot dog.

3 Victoria는 소파 위에 앉아 있지 않다. (sit)

= Victoria _____ _____ _____ on the sofa.

4 그 아이는 문 뒤에 숨어있니? (hide)

= _____ the child _____ behind the door?

5 너는 Ashley를 초대할 거니? (invite)

= _____ you _____ _____ _____ Ashley?

6 그들은 오늘 오후에 집에 있을 거니? (be)

= _____ they _____ at home this afternoon?

7 나의 부모님은 호수를 따라서 걷고 계신다. (walk)

= My parents _____ _____ along the lake.

B 우리말과 같도록 괄호 안의 말을 알맞게 배열하시오.

1 그들은 지금 그들의 숙제를 하고 있지 않다. (not, are, they, doing)

= _____ their homework now.

2 너는 오늘 밤에 너의 오빠에게 사과할 거니? (apologize, you, will)

= _____ to your brother tonight?

3 그 소녀들은 택시를 타지 않을 것이다. (are, the girls, going to, not, take)

= _____ a taxi.

4 그 쇼핑몰은 다음 주말에 문을 열지 않을 것이다. (the mall, not, will, open)

= _____ next weekend.

5 너와 너의 친구는 무언가를 요리하고 있니? (cooking, you and your friend, are)

= _____ something?

C 다음 그림을 보고 괄호 안의 말을 활용하여 대화를 완성하시오.

1    2   3    4

1 *A*: Is Bella feeding her dog now?

　B: No, ＿＿＿＿＿＿＿＿＿＿. ＿＿＿＿＿＿＿＿＿＿＿＿＿ her dog now. (wash)

2 *A*: ＿＿＿＿＿＿＿＿＿＿＿＿＿ at a bookstore? (Mr. Brown, work)

　B: No, ＿＿＿＿＿＿＿＿＿. He is working at a café.

3 *A*: ＿＿＿＿＿＿＿＿＿＿＿＿＿ in the classroom? (the students, sit)

　B: Yes, ＿＿＿＿＿＿＿＿. They are waiting for their teacher.

4 *A*: Is he driving the car?

　B: No, ＿＿＿＿＿＿＿＿＿. ＿＿＿＿＿＿＿＿＿＿＿＿＿ the car. (fix)

D 괄호 안의 말을 활용하여 대화를 완성하시오.

> *Jane*: Do you have a vacation plan?
>
> *Sean*: Yes. I ⓐ＿＿＿＿＿＿＿＿＿＿＿ 20 books. (be going to, read)
>
> *Jane*: Sounds interesting. My sister and I ⓑ＿＿＿＿＿＿＿＿＿＿＿ to Europe.
> (be going to, travel) We will visit Italy and Germany.
>
> *Sean*: ⓒ＿＿＿＿＿ you ＿＿＿＿＿ France, too? (will, visit)
>
> *Jane*: No, we won't. And my sister ⓓ＿＿＿＿＿＿＿＿＿＿＿ YouTube Videos there.
> (be going to, make)
>
> *Sean*: Wow, I ⓔ＿＿＿＿＿＿＿＿＿＿＿ her videos! (will, watch)

Chapter 06

현재진행시제와 미래시제

Hackers Grammar Smart Starter

Chapter Test

[1-2] 다음 중 동사의 V-ing형이 <u>잘못된</u> 것을 고르시오.

1 ① take – taking ② tie – tying
③ climb – climbing ④ run – runing
⑤ study – studying

2 ① buy – buying ② learn – learning
③ give – giveing ④ put – putting
⑤ lie – lying

[3-4] 다음 빈칸에 들어갈 알맞은 것을 고르시오.

3

> Jessica _____ return the book tomorrow.

① is ② be ③ are
④ will ⑤ do

4

> _____ the kids playing in the sand now?

① Is ② Are ③ Will
④ Do ⑤ Does

5 다음 빈칸에 들어갈 말로 <u>어색한</u> 것을 <u>모두</u> 고르시오.

> We are going to eat salad _____.

① yesterday ② tomorrow ③ last night
④ soon ⑤ next Monday

6 다음 빈칸에 들어갈 말이 나머지 넷과 <u>다른</u> 것은?

① The ducks _____ swimming in the pond.
② They _____ watching a movie now.
③ Erica and I _____ making some cookies.
④ My sisters _____ planning a trip.
⑤ The soup _____ boiling in the pot.

서술형

[7-8] 다음 빈칸에 알맞은 말을 넣어 질문에 대한 대답을 완성하시오.

7

> *A*: Are you and Mason going to visit the temple next weekend?
> *B*: Yes, _____ _____.

8

> *A*: Is Amy planting flowers?
> *B*: No, _____ _____.

[9-10] 다음 중 밑줄 친 부분이 어법상 <u>어색한</u> 것을 고르시오.

9 ① Natalie <u>isn't reading</u> a newspaper.
② The boy <u>is choosing</u> a new toy.
③ Are they <u>talking</u> to Mr. Parker now?
④ Is this computer <u>working</u> well?
⑤ They <u>not are cleaning</u> the window.

10 ① Are you <u>going to raise</u> a pet?

② He <u>won't listens</u> to me.

③ <u>Will</u> Jane <u>leave</u> home at 7:30?

④ Kate <u>isn't going to buy</u> the shoes.

⑤ The doctor <u>will call</u> your name soon.

11 다음 빈칸에 공통으로 들어갈 알맞은 것은?

> • _____ you going to drink hot chocolate?
> • The students _____ singing a song.

① be   ② is   ③ are

④ will   ⑤ do

[고난도]

12 다음 빈칸에 들어갈 말이 순서대로 짝지어진 것은?

> • Fred _____ sitting on the bench now.
>   He is jogging on the track.
> • My sister and I are _____ the cats.

① is – feed   ② is not – feed

③ is – feeding   ④ is not – feeding

⑤ is not – will feed

[서술형] [고난도]

[13-15] 우리말과 같도록 괄호 안의 말을 활용하여 빈칸에 쓰시오.

13

> 오늘 밤에 비가 오지 않을 것이다. (it, rain)

= _____ _____ _____ _____

tonight.

14

> 그녀는 눈사람을 만들고 있니? (make)

= _____ _____ _____ a snowman?

15

> 그들은 내일 미술 수업을 듣지 않을 것이다. (take)

= _____ _____ _____

_____ _____ the art class tomorrow.

[서술형]

[16-18] 우리말과 같도록 괄호 안의 말을 알맞게 배열하시오.

16

> Anna는 일주일 동안 런던에 머무를 거니? (Anna, is, stay, going to)

= _____ in London for

a week?

17

> 나는 그 문제에 대해 생각하고 있지 않다. (not, I, thinking, am)

= _____ about the

problem.

18

> 너는 그에게 너의 자전거를 팔 거니? (sell, will, your bicycle, you)

= _____ to him?

Word Review

Chapter 06에 나온 어휘 중 잘 외워지지 않는 것은 박스에 체크하여 복습하시오.

☐ draw	동 그리다	☐ field trip	현장 학습
☐ tie	동 묶다	☐ fun	형 재미있는; 명 재미
☐ magazine	명 잡지	☐ promise	명 약속; 동 약속하다
☐ tell	동 말하다	☐ order	동 주문하다
☐ die	동 죽다	☐ hide	동 숨다
☐ wear	동 입다	☐ along	전 ~을 따라서
☐ living room	거실	☐ apologize	동 사과하다
☐ take a picture	사진을 찍다	☐ feed	동 먹이다
☐ exam	명 시험	☐ return	동 반납하다
☐ musical instrument	악기	☐ pot	명 냄비
☐ glue	명 접착제, 풀	☐ choose	동 선택하다
☐ pack	동 (짐 등을) 싸다	☐ raise	동 키우다, 기르다
☐ paint	동 페인트를 칠하다	☐ track	명 길, 경주로
☐ truth	명 사실	☐ think	동 생각하다
☐ rain	동 비가 오다	☐ sell	동 팔다

Check-up

영어 어휘와 알맞은 우리말 뜻을 연결하시오.

1 die   ·   · ⓐ 시험
2 exam   ·   · ⓑ 죽다
3 pack   ·   · ⓒ 키우다, 기르다
4 raise   ·   · ⓓ 냄비
5 pot   ·   · ⓔ (짐 등을) 싸다

6 tie   ·   · ⓐ 묶다
7 field trip ·   · ⓑ 주문하다
8 order   ·   · ⓒ 비가 오다
9 rain   ·   · ⓓ 현장 학습
10 think   ·   · ⓔ 생각하다

정답 1 ⓑ 2 ⓐ 3 ⓔ 4 ⓒ 5 ⓓ 6 ⓐ 7 ⓓ 8 ⓑ 9 ⓒ 10 ⓔ

Chapter

07

조동사

조동사는 be동사나 일반동사와 함께 쓰여 여러 가지 의미를 더하는 말이다.

UNIT 01 | can, may

1 조동사

be동사나 일반동사와 함께 쓰여 능력, 허가, 추측, 의무 등의 의미를 더하는 말로, 「조동사 + 동사원형」의 형태로 쓴다. 조동사는 주어의 인칭이나 수에 따라 형태가 변하지 않는다.

Koalas **can** *climb* a tree.
I **must** *do* the laundry.

2 can

❶ 능력·가능(~할 수 있다)

She **can** drive a truck.
Can he climb a tree?

※ cannot[can't]: ~할 수 없다
　 Ross **cannot[can't]** eat spicy food.

❷ 허가(~해도 된다)

You **can** read my book.
Can I ask a question?

3 may

❶ 허가(~해도 된다)

You **may** play outside.
May I wear the hat?

❷ 추측(~일지도 모른다)

The dog **may** be in the bathroom.
It **may** rain soon.

Smart Check 주어진 문장을 우리말로 해석하시오.

1 Sam can speak French. = Sam은 프랑스어를 _____.

2 May I close the window? = 내가 창문을 _____?

3 You can go now. = 너는 지금 _____.

4 She may be sad. = 그녀는 _____.

Practice

Answers p.9

A 괄호 안에서 가장 알맞은 것을 고르시오.

1 You can (stay / staying) at my house.

2 Ms. Jones (can / cans) bake bread.

3 The baby may (is / be) hungry now.

4 You (return may / may return) my pen tomorrow.

5 Tom (not can / cannot) play the flute.

6 May (I see / see I) your new bag?

7 (May / Can) you open this bottle?

stay 툉 머무르다
bake 툉 굽다
return 툉 돌려주다, 반납하다

B 다음 대화의 빈칸에 알맞은 말을 <보기>에서 한 번씩만 골라 쓰시오.

> <보기>   can   cannot   may

1 A: I _____ solve this problem.
B: Don't worry. Mr. Watson will help you.

2 A: They exercised too hard in the morning.
B: Yes. They _____ feel tired this afternoon.

3 A: Alice _____ sing very well.
B: Yes. She was the winner of a singing contest.

solve 툉 풀다, 해결하다
worry 툉 걱정하다
too 閈 너무
winner 囤 우승자
contest 囤 대회

C 다음 그림을 보고 <보기>의 말과 괄호 안의 동사를 한 번씩만 활용하여 문장을 완성하시오.

snow 툉 눈이 오다; 囤 눈
use 툉 사용하다

1  **2**  **3**

> <보기>   can   cannot   may

1 It _____ tomorrow. (snow)

2 The girl _____ the Internet. (use)

3 Matthew _____ well. (ski)

Chapter 07 조동사 **81**

UNIT 02 | must, have to

1 must

의무(~해야 한다)를 나타낸다.

I **must** feed my dog.
The children **must** wear life jackets.

※ must not: 강한 금지(~하면 안 된다)
  Visitors **must not** take photos here.

---

2 have to

의무(~해야 한다)를 나타내며, must와 바꿔 쓸 수 있다. 주어가 3인칭 단수일 때는 has to를 쓴다.

You **have to** be quiet in the hospital.
We **have to** protect forests.

She **has to** wear a helmet.
Bruce **has to** fix his laptop.

※ don't/doesn't have to: 불필요(~할 필요가 없다)
  I **don't have to** meet Doris.
  He **doesn't have to** go to school today.

TIP **must not**(~하면 안 된다)과 **don't/doesn't have to**(~할 필요가 없다)의 의미 차이에 주의한다.
  You **must not** push this button. <강한 금지>
  You **don't have to** push this button. <불필요>

Smart Check 주어진 문장을 우리말로 해석하시오.

1 Logan must wake up early.   = Logan은 일찍 _____.

2 They must not sit on this bench.   = 그들은 이 벤치에 _____.

3 We have to wait.   = 우리는 _____.

4 She doesn't have to buy onions.   = 그녀는 양파를 _____.

Practice

Answers p.9

A 괄호 안에서 가장 알맞은 것을 고르시오.

1 She must (show / shows) her ID card.

2 I (have / have to) call my mom after class.

3 We (must not / not must) lie to our parents.

4 Helen (has / have) to finish her meal.

5 Jake (don't / doesn't) have to see the doctor.

6 You (must not / don't have to) hurry. You have much time.

show 통 보여주다
ID card 신분증
lie 통 거짓말하다
meal 명 식사
see the doctor 병원에 가다
hurry 통 서두르다

B 다음 그림을 보고 must 또는 must not과 <보기>의 동사를 활용하여 문장을 완성하시오.

1    **2**    **3**

loudly 부 큰 소리로

| <보기> | wash | talk | ride |

1 You _____ a bicycle here.

2 You _____ your hands.

3 You _____ loudly.

C 우리말과 같도록 have to와 괄호 안의 동사를 활용하여 문장을 완성하시오.

1 나는 저 버스를 타야 한다. (take)

= I _____ that bus.

2 그들은 그들의 미래에 대해 걱정할 필요가 없다. (worry)

= They _____ about their future.

3 그는 오늘 집에 걸어가야 한다. (walk)

= He _____ home today.

4 Jessie는 그 파티를 준비할 필요가 없다. (prepare)

= Jessie _____ for the party.

future 명 미래
prepare for ~을 준비하다

Chapter 07

조동사

Hackers Grammar Smart Starter

Writing Exercise

A 다음 문장의 밑줄 친 부분을 바르게 고쳐 쓰시오.

1 Kelly <u>musts</u> start her vacation homework.　　→ _____

2 James has to <u>says</u> sorry to Erica.　　→ _____

3 Can <u>run you</u> fast?　　→ _____

4 He <u>don't have to</u> download the file.　　→ _____

5 May I <u>drinking</u> some milk?　　→ _____

6 I <u>not can</u> find my glasses.　　→ _____

7 You <u>not have to</u> make lunch. I ordered some food.　　→ _____

B 우리말과 같도록 괄호 안의 동사를 활용하여 빈칸에 쓰시오.

1 너는 이 강에서 낚시하면 안 된다. (fish)

= You _____ _____ _____ in this river.

2 Mary는 그녀의 지갑을 찾아야 한다. (find)

= Mary _____ _____ _____ her wallet.

3 내가 여기에 나의 가방을 놓아도 되니? (put)

= _____ I _____ my bag here?

4 우리는 콘서트에 늦을지도 모른다. (be)

= We _____ _____ late for the concert.

5 너는 에어컨을 켜도 된다. (turn)

= You _____ _____ on the air conditioner.

6 학생들은 그들의 선생님 말씀을 주의 깊게 들어야 한다. (listen)

= Students _____ _____ to their teacher carefully.

C 우리말과 같도록 괄호 안의 말을 알맞게 배열하시오.

1 너는 넥타이를 맬 필요가 없다. (wear, to, a tie, don't, you, have)

= _____.

2 Alan은 그 책을 반납해야 한다. (return, Alan, the book, must)

= _____.

3 내가 너의 휴대폰을 빌려도 되니? (I, your cell phone, borrow, may)

= _____?

4 너는 젓가락을 사용할 수 있니? (use, can, chopsticks, you)

= _____?

5 Megan과 나는 식탁을 닦아야 한다. (Megan and I, to, the table, clean, have)

= _____.

6 그의 삼촌은 세 개의 언어를 말할 수 있다. (speak, his uncle, three languages, can)

= _____.

D 다음 그림을 보고 <보기>의 동사와 괄호 안의 말을 활용하여 문장을 완성하시오.

1

2

3

4

| <보기> | be | water | reach | run |

1 Laura is short. She _____ the book. (can)

2 The students _____. The floor is slippery. (must)

3 The boy is wearing a soccer uniform. He _____ in the soccer club. (may)

4 You _____ the trees. It will rain soon. (have to)

Chapter Test

[1-4] 다음 빈칸에 들어갈 가장 알맞은 것을 고르시오.

1

I _____ speak Spanish. I studied it for two years.

① can   ② cannot   ③ don't have to
④ may   ⑤ must not

2

Maria _____ be in the kitchen. She was cooking five minutes ago.

① can   ② cannot   ③ may
④ must not   ⑤ doesn't have to

3

You _____ touch the frying pan. It's hot.

① can   ② may   ③ must
④ must not   ⑤ don't have to

4

We _____ hurry. The class will start soon.

① can   ② may   ③ have to
④ must not   ⑤ don't have to

고난도

5 다음 중 밑줄 친 부분의 의미가 나머지 넷과 다른 것은?

① We <u>can</u> help the poor children.
② Jason <u>can</u> swim in the ocean.
③ I <u>can</u> remember your name.
④ You <u>can</u> go home now.
⑤ They <u>can</u> play the board game.

서술형

[6-8] 다음 빈칸에 가장 알맞은 말을 <보기>에서 한 번씩만 골라 쓰시오.

<보기>   may   must not   don't have to

6

You _____ have my sweater. It is too small for me.

7

I _____ go to bed early today. It is Sunday tomorrow.

8

We _____ cross the street. The traffic light is red.

고난도

[9-10] 다음 대화의 빈칸에 들어갈 말이 순서대로 짝지어진 것을 고르시오.

9

A: _____ I use this cup?
B: Yes. But you _____ wash it first. It is dirty.

① May – can   ② May – have to
③ Can – may   ④ Can – don't have to
⑤ Must – can

10

A: I _____ buy my train ticket.

B: You _____ buy it. I already bought it for you.

① must – don't have to ② have to – must

③ must – must ④ have to – cannot

⑤ may – don't have to

[11-12] 다음 중 밑줄 친 부분이 어법상 어색한 것을 고르시오.

11 ① The dog can't jump high.

② You may stay in this room.

③ Derek can rides a roller coaster.

④ May I ask a question?

⑤ Can you put this on the table?

12 ① You must rest at home.

② I have to borrow an umbrella.

③ We must not walk on the grass.

④ Jack don't have to take the test.

⑤ Kelly has to go to the supermarket.

서술형

[13-14] 다음 문장에서 어법상 어색한 부분을 찾아 쓰고 바르게 고쳐 쓰시오.

13

Dad may comes home early today.

_____ → _____

14

You not must drink coffee.

_____ → _____

서술형

[15-18] 우리말과 같도록 괄호 안의 말을 활용하여 문장을 완성하시오.

15

그 이야기는 사실일지도 모른다. (be true)

= The story _____.

16

너는 지금 샤워를 해야 한다. (take a shower)

= You _____ now.

17

나는 이 수학 문제를 풀 수 없다. (solve this math problem)

= I _____.

18

우리는 플라스틱을 사용하면 안 된다. (use plastics)

= We _____.

Word Review

Chapter 07에 나온 어휘 중 잘 외워지지 않는 것은 박스에 체크하여 복습하시오.

□ laundry	명 빨래	□ carefully	부 조심스럽게
□ close	동 닫다	□ chopstick	명 젓가락
□ solve	동 풀다, 해결하다	□ language	명 언어
□ problem	명 문제	□ reach	동 ~에 닿다, 이르다
□ worry	동 걱정하다	□ floor	명 바닥
□ protect	동 보호하다	□ slippery	형 미끄러운
□ fix	동 고치다	□ touch	동 만지다
□ wait	동 기다리다	□ poor	형 가난한, 불쌍한
□ lie	동 거짓말하다	□ ocean	명 바다
□ future	명 미래	□ cross	동 건너다
□ prepare for	~을 준비하다	□ traffic light	신호등
□ find	동 찾다	□ first	부 우선, 먼저
□ fish	동 낚시하다; 명 물고기	□ dirty	형 더러운
□ river	명 강	□ already	부 이미, 벌써
□ turn on	(전기, 기계 등을) 켜다	□ true	형 사실인, 맞는

Check-up

영어 어휘와 알맞은 우리말 뜻을 연결하시오.

1 traffic light · · ⓐ 신호등
2 floor · · ⓑ 바닥
3 prepare for · · ⓒ 미래
4 future · · ⓓ ~을 준비하다
5 protect · · ⓔ 보호하다

6 true · · ⓐ 찾다
7 laundry · · ⓑ 사실인, 맞는
8 reach · · ⓒ 빨래
9 already · · ⓓ ~에 닿다, 이르다
10 find · · ⓔ 이미, 벌써

정답 1ⓐ 2ⓑ 3ⓓ 4ⓒ 5ⓔ 6ⓑ 7ⓒ 8ⓓ 9ⓔ 10ⓐ

Chapter

08

동사의 종류

동사의 종류에 따라 필수 문장 요소가 달라진다.

UNIT 01 | 감각동사

1 감각동사

'보이다, 들리다, 냄새가 나다' 등의 감각을 나타내는 동사이다.

look ~하게 보이다	sound ~하게 들리다	smell ~한 냄새가 나다
taste ~한 맛이 나다	feel ~하게 느끼다	

He **looks** happy.
Your idea **sounds** good.
This bread **smells** delicious.
The steak **tastes** salty.
I **feel** hungry.

2 감각동사가 있는 문장

「주어 + 감각동사 + 주격 보어」의 형태로 쓴다. 주격 보어는 주어를 보충 설명하는 말로, 감각동사의 주격 보어 자리에는 형용사만 온다.

Paul **looked** *sick*.
Her voice **sounds** *lovely*.
↳ lovely나 friendly처럼 -ly로 끝나서 부사처럼 보이지만 형용사인 단어에 주의한다.

The fish **smells** *bad*.
Strawberries **taste** *sweet*.
They **felt** *hot*.

TIP 감각동사 뒤에 명사가 올 때는 전치사 **like**와 함께 「감각동사 + **like** + 명사」의 형태로 쓴다. 이때 전치사 **like**는 '~처럼, ~ 같이'라는 의미이다.
The noise **sounded like** *thunder*.
My tea **tastes like** *peaches*.

Smart Check 다음 빈칸에 들어갈 알맞은 것을 고르시오.

1 I felt _____ yesterday.
① sad   ② sadly

2 Your song sounded _____.
① beauty   ② beautiful

3 The puppy _____ a doll.
① looks   ② looks like

Practice

A 괄호 안에서 알맞은 것을 고르시오.

1 I feel (great / greatly) today.

2 Your voice (sounds / looks) strange.

3 My teacher looks (friend / friendly).

4 Lemons (taste / sound) sour.

5 This flower smells (good / well).

6 The cracker (smelled / smelled like) cheese.

voice 몡 목소리
strange 혱 이상한
sour 혱 신
cracker 몡 크래커

B 다음 빈칸에 알맞은 말을 <보기>에서 한 번씩만 골라 쓰시오.

| <보기> looks like   sounds   tastes   feels |

1 The sofa _____ comfortable.

2 This sauce _____ spicy.

3 Sandra _____ her mother.

4 His plan _____ interesting.

comfortable 혱 편안한
sauce 몡 소스
spicy 혱 매운
plan 몡 계획
interesting 혱 흥미로운

C 다음 그림을 보고 <보기>의 동사와 괄호 안의 말을 한 번씩만 활용하여 빈칸에 쓰시오. (단, 현재형으로 쓰시오.)

1  2  3

fruit 몡 과일
terrible 혱 끔찍한
lake 몡 호수
peaceful 혱 평화로운

| <보기>   look   smell   taste |

1 This fruit _____ _____. (terrible)

2 The juice _____ _____ _____ _____. (an orange)

3 The lake _____ _____. (peaceful)

UNIT 02 | 수여동사

1 수여동사

'-에게 ~을 (해)주다'라는 의미를 나타내는 동사이다.

give -에게 ~을 주다	send -에게 ~을 보내주다	bring -에게 ~을 가져다주다
pass -에게 ~을 건네주다	show -에게 ~을 보여주다	teach -에게 ~을 가르쳐주다
tell -에게 ~을 말해주다	write -에게 ~을 써주다	read -에게 ~을 읽어주다
lend -에게 ~을 빌려주다	buy -에게 ~을 사주다	cook -에게 ~을 요리해주다
find -에게 ~을 찾아주다	make -에게 ~을 만들어주다	get -에게 ~을 가져다주다
build -에게 ~을 만들어주다	ask -에게 ~을 묻다	

Gary **passed** Betty the sugar.
My dad **cooked** me breakfast.
I **made** him a paper boat.
Ms. Call **built** her son a snowman.

2 수여동사가 있는 문장

「주어 + 수여동사 + 간접 목적어(-에게) + 직접 목적어(~을)」의 형태로 쓴다.

I **gave** *Rebecca the books*.
Mark will **buy** *his friend snacks*.
She **asked** *the teacher a question*.

> **TIP** 「주어 + 수여동사 + 간접 목적어 + 직접 목적어」는 「주어 + 수여동사 + 직접 목적어 + **to/for/of** + 간접 목적어」로 바꿔 쓸 수 있다. 이때 쓰는 전치사 to/for/of는 동사에 따라 다르다.
>
> | to를 쓰는 동사 | give, send, bring, pass, show, teach, tell, write, read, lend 등 |
> |---|---|
> | for를 쓰는 동사 | buy, cook, find, make, get, build 등 |
> | of를 쓰는 동사 | ask 등 |

I **gave** *the books* **to** *Rebecca*.
Mark will **buy** *snacks* **for** *his friend*.
She **asked** *a question* **of** *the teacher*.

Smart Check 다음 빈칸에 들어갈 알맞은 것을 고르시오.

1 He told _____.
　① the rumor us　② us the rumor

2 My grandfather made a toy _____ me.
　① to　② for

Practice

A

<보기>와 같이 다음 문장의 간접 목적어에는 동그라미를 치고, 직접 목적어에는 밑줄을 치시오.

<보기>	He showed (me) a picture.

1 I sent Alice an e-mail.

2 The server got them napkins.

3 She lent her classmate textbooks.

4 Mom brought me the lunch box.

5 Thomas bought his girlfriend a teddy bear.

server 뗑 종업원
napkin 뗑 냅킨
classmate 뗑 반 친구
textbook 뗑 교과서
lunch box 도시락
teddy bear 곰 인형

B

다음 빈칸에 알맞은 동사를 <보기>에서 한 번씩만 골라 쓰시오. (단, 과거형으로 쓰시오.)

<보기>	show	teach	write	cook	ask

1 Ms. Bell _____ math to students.

2 Joshua _____ the staff some questions.

3 He _____ us his puppy yesterday.

4 I _____ my parents a letter on Parents' Day.

5 The chef _____ tomato pasta for us.

math 뗑 수학
staff 뗑 직원
puppy 뗑 강아지
Parents' Day 어버이날
chef 뗑 요리사

C

다음 그림을 보고 괄호 안의 말을 알맞게 배열하시오.

1  **2**  **3**

fairy tale 동화
present 뗑 선물
sandcastle 뗑 모래성

1 Dad _____ at night. (me, reads, a fairy tale)

2 Santa Claus _____. (to, presents, the kids, gave)

3 John _____. (a sandcastle, his brother, built)

Chapter 08

동사의 종류

Hackers Grammar Smart **Starter**

Writing Exercise

A   우리말과 같도록 괄호 안의 말을 알맞게 배열하시오.

1 이 채소는 쓴 맛이 난다. (bitter, tastes)

= This vegetable _____.

2 Jenny의 오빠는 그녀에게 그 소스를 건네줬다. (her, passed, the sauce)

= Jenny's brother _____.

3 우리는 그 이웃들에게 우리의 집을 보여줬다. (showed, to, our house, the neighbors)

= We _____.

4 그의 방은 항상 깨끗해 보인다. (clean, looks)

= His room always _____.

5 저것은 약 같은 냄새가 난다. (medicine, like, smells)

= That _____.

6 Charlie는 나에게 물 한 잔을 가져다줬다. (a glass of water, me, for, got)

= Charlie _____.

B   우리말과 같도록 괄호 안의 말을 활용하여 빈칸에 쓰시오.

1 햇빛은 따뜻하게 느껴진다. (feel, warm)

= The sunlight _____ _____.

2 나의 사촌은 나에게 질문을 했다. (ask, a question)

= My cousin _____ _____ _____ _____.

3 저 바위는 거북처럼 보인다. (look, a turtle)

= That rock _____ _____ _____ _____.

4 그 라디오는 어제 크게 들렸다. (sound, loud)

= The radio _____ _____.

5 Smith씨는 우리에게 정원을 만들어주셨다. (build, a garden)

= Mr. Smith _____ _____ _____ _____ _____.

6 Sharon은 그에게 이메일을 보내줬다. (send, an e-mail)

= Sharon _____ _____ _____ _____.

C 다음 대화의 빈칸에 알맞은 말을 <보기>에서 한 번씩만 골라 쓰시오.

<보기>	sounds like	feels	wrote	lent	bought

1 *A*: Can I borrow your eraser?

   B: Sorry. I _____ it to Teresa.

2 *A*: This raincoat still _____ wet.

   B: You have to dry it outside.

3 *A*: Ms. Turner looks very happy today.

   B: That's because her husband _____ her a poem.

4 *A*: My father _____ me this phone last week.

   B: It looks so cool.

5 *A*: Tiffany and I will go on a picnic this weekend.

   B: That _____ a good idea.

D 다음 그림을 보고 <보기>의 동사와 괄호 안의 말을 활용하여 빈칸에 쓰시오. (단, 과거형으로 쓰시오.)

  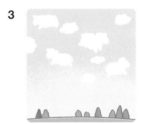 

<보기>	look	sound	give	make

1 His violin performance _____ _____. (sad)

2 The teacher _____ _____ _____ _____. (Sally, an award)

3 The clouds _____ _____ _____. (sheep)

4 She _____ _____ _____ _____ _____. (her son, gloves)

[1-3] 다음 빈칸에 들어갈 말로 <u>어색한</u> 것을 <u>모두</u> 고르시오.

1

The shampoo smells _____.

① nice ② wonderfully ③ bad
④ sweet ⑤ flowers

2

The teacher will _____ us lunch.

① buy ② feel ③ look
④ bring ⑤ cook

3

That orange _____ sour.

① makes ② tastes ③ looks
④ smells ⑤ shows

서술형

[4-6] 다음 빈칸에 알맞은 말을 <보기>에서 한 번씩만 골라 쓰시오.

<보기> tasted   felt   lent

4

Peter _____ hungry in the mornig.

5

Hanna _____ her sister a red jacket.

6

The cake _____ like chocolate.

[7-9] 다음 중 밑줄 친 부분이 어법상 <u>어색한</u> 것을 고르시오.

7 ① The boy <u>looks friendly</u>.
② The bread <u>smelled delicious</u>.
③ Your hands always <u>smell good</u>.
④ Ms. Brown <u>sounded angrily</u>.
⑤ I <u>felt terrible</u> about the news.

8 ① David <u>wrote a letter to Chloe</u>.
② I will <u>show you a video clip</u>.
③ Mom <u>told a story me</u> last night.
④ They <u>cooked Chinese food for the children</u>.
⑤ Mr. Williams <u>asked us a question</u>.

9 ① Erica <u>gave her bracelet to Janet</u>.
② His plan <u>sounded perfect</u>.
③ Sam <u>bought a new ball for his brother</u>.
④ The woman <u>looked a doctor</u>.
⑤ He <u>built his nephew a toy house</u>.

고난도

[10-11] 다음 대화의 빈칸에 들어갈 말이 순서대로 짝지어진 것을 고르시오.

10

> A: Ricky _____ me a gift.
> B: Wow, that box looks _____!

① taught – heavy　② read – heavy
③ gave – heavy　④ read – heavily
⑤ gave – heavily

11

> A: The pancakes _____ butter.
> B: Josh made them _____ you and me.

① sound like – for　② smell like – to
③ sound – to　④ smell like – for
⑤ smell – for

12 다음 빈칸에 like가 들어갈 수 있는 것을 <u>모두</u> 고르시오.

① The candy tastes _____ bananas.
② I feel _____ cold now.
③ This soap smells _____ great.
④ The door bell sounds _____ scary.
⑤ The shadow looks _____ a lion.

서술형

[13-14] 우리말과 같도록 괄호 안의 말을 알맞게 배열하시오.

13

> 그 활동은 나에게 흥미진진하게 보인다. (exciting, looks)

= The activity _____ to me.

14

> Matt은 그의 친구에게 비밀을 말해줬다. (his friend, told, a secret)

= Matt _____.

서술형　고난도

[15-17] 우리말과 같도록 괄호 안의 말을 활용하여 빈칸에 쓰시오.

15

> 그는 나에게 그 종이를 건네줬다. (the paper)

= He _____ _____ _____
_____ _____.

16

> Jake는 운동 후에 피곤하게 느꼈다. (tired)

= Jake _____ _____ after the exercise.

17

> 나는 그녀에게 신발 한 짝을 찾아줬다. (a shoe)

= I _____ _____ _____ _____.

Word Review

Chapter 08에 나온 어휘 중 잘 외워지지 않는 것은 박스에 체크하여 복습하시오.

☐ voice	몡 목소리	☐ sandcastle	몡 모래성
☐ friendly	혱 친절한	☐ vegetable	몡 채소
☐ noise	몡 소리, 소음	☐ warm	혱 따뜻한
☐ thunder	몡 천둥	☐ turtle	몡 거북
☐ sour	혱 신	☐ still	붜 아직
☐ comfortable	혱 편안한	☐ poem	몡 시
☐ sauce	몡 소스	☐ performance	몡 공연, 연주회
☐ interesting	혱 흥미로운	☐ award	몡 상
☐ terrible	혱 끔찍한	☐ wonderfully	붜 아주, 아주 잘
☐ peaceful	혱 평화로운	☐ bracelet	몡 팔찌
☐ math	몡 수학	☐ soap	몡 비누
☐ staff	몡 직원	☐ shadow	몡 그림자
☐ chef	몡 요리사	☐ exciting	혱 흥미진진한
☐ fairy tale	동화	☐ activity	몡 활동
☐ present	몡 선물	☐ secret	몡 비밀

Check-up

영어 어휘와 알맞은 우리말 뜻을 연결하시오.

1	chef	·	· ⓐ 팔찌
2	terrible	·	· ⓑ 요리사
3	bracelet	·	· ⓒ 소리, 소음
4	vegetable	·	· ⓓ 끔찍한
5	noise	·	· ⓔ 채소

6	still	·	· ⓐ 친절한
7	exciting	·	· ⓑ 흥미진진한
8	math	·	· ⓒ 아직
9	fairy tale	·	· ⓓ 동화
10	friendly	·	· ⓔ 수학

정답 1ⓑ 2ⓓ 3ⓐ 4ⓔ 5ⓒ 6ⓒ 7ⓑ 8ⓔ 9ⓓ 10ⓐ

Chapter

09

전치사

전치사는 명사나 대명사 앞에 와서 장소나 시간 등을 나타내는 말이다.

UNIT 01 | 장소를 나타내는 전치사

1 전치사

❶ 전치사는 명사나 대명사 앞에 와서 장소나 시간 등을 나타낸다.

The vase is **on** the table.
I met him **in** March.

❷ 전치사 뒤에 인칭대명사가 올 때는 목적격을 쓴다.

My dog followed **behind** me.
The baby is sleeping **next to** her.

2 at(~에, ~에서), in(~ 안에, ~에)

at	비교적 좁은 장소나 하나의 지점	**at** home **at** the airport	**at** school **at** the station
in	도시, 국가 등 비교적 넓은 장소나 공간의 내부	**in** Seoul **in** the bag	**in** Canada **in** the room

They are **at** home now.
The bus stopped **at** the station.

Dorothy arrived **in** New York.
There are two cats **in** the box.

3 on(~ 위에, ~에), under(~ 아래에)

on은 표면에 접촉하여 위에 있는 상태를 나타내고, under는 표면과 떨어져서 아래에 있는 상태를 나타낸다.

He put the phone **on** the bed.
There was a bird **under** the bridge.

4 in front of(~ 앞에), behind(~ 뒤에), next to(~ 옆에)

She cried **in front of** us.
The parking lot is **behind** the building.
I will sit **next to** Jane.

 다음 빈칸에 들어갈 알맞은 것을 고르시오.

1 My sister is behind _____ .

   ① he   ② him

2 Edward stayed _____ his room.

   ① on   ② in

Practice

A 괄호 안에서 알맞은 것을 고르시오.

1 His house is (on / in) the hill.

2 They are standing behind (we / us).

3 My dad is (at / in) the garden.

4 There is a mirror (next / next to) the closet.

5 Amy met Steve (at / on) school.

hill 뗑 언덕
stand 통 서 있다, 서다
mirror 뗑 거울
closet 뗑 벽장

B 다음 그림을 보고 빈칸에 알맞은 전치사를 <보기>에서 골라 쓰시오.

<보기>	in	on	under	in front of	behind

1 There is a clock _____ the wall.

2 Mary's seat is _____ Jack.

3 The teacher is _____ the students.

4 There are four students _____ the classroom.

5 There is a pen _____ the chair.

clock 뗑 시계
wall 뗑 벽
seat 뗑 자리, 좌석
classroom 뗑 교실

C 우리말과 같도록 빈칸에 알맞은 전치사를 쓰시오.

1 내 앞에 키가 큰 남자가 있다.
   = There is a tall man _____ me.

2 Brian과 나는 작년에 이스탄불에 있었다.
   = Brian and I were _____ Istanbul last year.

3 그 옷가게는 우체국 옆에 있다.
   = The clothes store is _____ the post office.

4 그녀는 그 나무 아래에서 잠시 휴식을 취할 것이다.
   = She will take a break _____ the tree.

5 너희들은 공항에서 말썽을 일으키면 안 된다.
   = You must not make trouble _____ the airport.

tall 혱 키가 큰
clothes store 옷가게
post office 우체국
take a break 잠시 휴식을 취하다
make trouble 말썽을 일으키다

Chapter 09 전치사 Hackers Grammar Smart **Starter**

UNIT 02 | 시간을 나타내는 전치사

1 at, on, in(~에)

at	시각, 시점	**at** 11 o'clock **at** noon	**at** 6:30 **at** night	
on	요일, 날짜, 기념일	**on** Thursday **on** my birthday	**on** October 20 **on** Halloween	
in	월, 계절, 연도, 아침·오후·저녁	**in** June **in** the morning/afternoon/evening	**in** winter	**in** 1980

The meeting starts **at** 8 A.M.
I take a walk **at** noon.

He slept late **on** Sunday.
There is an event **on** New Year's Day.

Angela visited Busan **in** fall.
They will watch the news **in** the evening.

2 before(~ 전에), after(~ 후에)

Steven plays basketball **before** lunch.
We went to a bookstore **after** school.

3 for/during(~ 동안)

for 뒤에는 숫자를 포함한 기간 표현이 오고, during 뒤에는 특정 기간을 나타내는 명사가 온다.

for *ten minutes*, **for** *an hour*, **for** *three days*, **for** *two weeks*, **for** *a month*, **for** *20 years* 등
during *the vacation*, **during** *the holidays*, **during** *the game*, **during** *the summer* 등

She studied Italian **for** *two months*.
Some stores will close **during** *the holidays*.

Smart Check 다음 빈칸에 들어갈 알맞은 것을 고르시오.

1 I was happy _____ my birthday.
 ① at　　　　　 ② on

2 We have to make dinner _____ 8 P.M.
 ① before　　　 ② during

Practice

Answers p.11

A 다음 빈칸에 at, on, in 중 알맞은 것을 쓰시오.

1 _____ 3 o'clock

2 _____ February 11

3 _____ spring

4 _____ Children's Day

5 _____ the morning

6 _____ 2005

7 _____ Wednesday

8 _____ night

9 _____ July

10 _____ 5:15 P.M.

February 명 2월
spring 명 봄
Children's Day 어린이날
July 명 7월

B 괄호 안에서 알맞은 것을 고르시오.

1 It is very cold (for / during) the winter.

2 I always wash the dishes (on / after) dinner.

3 She came back home (in / before) midnight.

4 Anna will stay at my house (for / during) a week.

5 They usually eat snacks (in / at) the afternoon.

6 Ralph is going to go to the theme park (on / at) Saturday.

wash the dishes 설거지를 하다
midnight 명 자정
snack 명 간식
theme park 테마파크

C 우리말과 같도록 빈칸에 알맞은 전치사를 쓰시오.

1 Sarah는 아침 7시에 일어난다.

= Sarah gets up _____ 7 in the morning.

2 나는 3일 동안 그 책을 빌렸다.

= I borrowed the book _____ three days.

3 나의 아버지는 크리스마스 전에 선물을 준비하셨다.

= My father prepared a gift _____ Christmas.

4 일출 후에 갑자기 비가 왔다.

= It rained suddenly _____ sunrise.

5 그는 축구 경기 동안 다리를 다쳤다.

= He hurt his leg _____ the soccer game.

get up 일어나다
borrow 통 빌리다
prepare 통 준비하다
suddenly 문 갑자기
sunrise 명 일출

Writing Exercise

A 우리말과 같도록 빈칸에 알맞은 전치사를 <보기>에서 골라 쓰시오.

<보기>	at	under	behind

1 그 낯선 사람은 네 뒤에 있었다. = The stranger was _____ you.

2 나는 기차역에서 나의 반 친구를 봤다. = I saw my classmate _____ the train station.

3 Michael은 벽장 아래에서 동전 한 개를 찾았다. = Michael found a coin _____ the closet.

<보기>	on	in	after

4 나뭇잎은 가을에 빨갛게 변한다. = Leaves turn red _____ autumn.

5 그들은 야구 경기 후에 배가 고팠다. = They were hungry _____ the baseball game.

6 그녀는 밸런타인데이에 초콜릿을 만들었다. = She made chocolate _____ Valentine's Day.

B 우리말과 같도록 알맞은 전치사와 괄호 안의 말을 활용하여 문장을 완성하시오.

1 수학 시험은 11시 30분에 시작할 것이다. (11:30)
= The math test will start _____.

2 우리는 거울 앞에서 춤을 추고 있다. (the mirror)
= We are dancing _____.

3 Rebecca는 30분 동안 감자 수프를 만들었다. (30 minutes)
= Rebecca made potato soup _____.

4 지붕 위에 새들이 있다. (the roof)
= There are birds _____.

5 나의 사촌은 캐나다에서 자랐다. (Canada)
= My cousin grew up _____.

6 나는 주말 동안 그 박물관을 방문할 것이다. (the weekend)
= I'm going to visit the museum _____.

C 다음 그림을 보고 빈칸에 알맞은 전치사를 <보기>에서 골라 쓰시오.

<보기>	in	on	under	behind	next to

1 There are some tomatoes _____ the shopping cart.

2 There is a man _____ the shopping cart.

3 There is a wallet _____ the shopping cart.

4 The oranges are _____ the bananas.

5 The woman dropped an orange _____ the floor.

D 다음은 Emily의 어제 일정표이다. <보기>의 전치사와 괄호 안의 말을 활용하여 문장을 완성하시오.

8:00~8:30 A.M.	have breakfast
10:00~11:00 A.M.	do yoga
1:00~3:00 P.M.	read books
4:00~5:00 P.M.	take the violin lesson

<보기>	in	before	after	for

1 Emily had breakfast _____. (the morning)

2 Emily did yoga _____. (breakfast)

3 Emily read books _____. (the violin lesson)

4 Emily took the violin lesson _____. (an hour)

1 다음 빈칸에 들어갈 말로 <u>어색한</u> 것은?

My teacher is sitting next to _____.

① her ② I ③ Jack
④ the table ⑤ them

[2-4] 다음 빈칸에 들어갈 알맞은 것을 고르시오.

2
The Eiffel Tower is _____ Paris.

① at ② on ③ in
④ under ⑤ before

3
We go to school _____ 8 o'clock.

① at ② on ③ in
④ for ⑤ during

4
The movie will play _____ two hours.

① at ② on ③ behind
④ for ⑤ during

고난도
5 다음 빈칸에 공통으로 들어갈 알맞은 것은?

• Your hat may be _____ the table.
• Paula got a new laptop _____ her birthday.

① after ② at ③ on
④ behind ⑤ in

서술형
6 우리말과 같도록 빈칸에 알맞은 전치사를 쓰시오.

그 식당 앞에 탁자들과 의자들이 있다.

= There are tables and chairs _____ the restaurant.

서술형
[7-8] 다음 시간표를 보고 빈칸에 알맞은 전치사를 쓰시오.

Sports Lessons

Time \ Day	Monday	Wednesday	Friday
1 P.M.	tennis	yoga	X
3 P.M.	yoga	tennis	golf

7
On Monday, the yoga lesson starts _____ the tennis lesson.

8
On Friday, there isn't a lesson _____ the golf lesson.

9 다음 우리말을 알맞게 영작한 것은?

Eric은 버스 정류장에 일찍 도착했다.

① Eric arrived early at the bus stop.
② Eric arrived early on the bus stop.
③ Eric arrived early in front of the bus stop.
④ Eric arrived early before the bus stop.
⑤ Eric arrived early for the bus stop.

[10-11] 다음 빈칸에 들어갈 말이 나머지 넷과 다른 것을 고르시오.

10 ① I met my friend _____ 9:30.
② Serena went to the library _____ noon.
③ The plane leaves _____ 7 o'clock.
④ The concert ended _____ midnight.
⑤ George reads books _____ the evening.

11 ① We have to wait for him _____ an hour.
② Hanna took a shower _____ 15 minutes.
③ Mr. Hart will close his store _____ two months.
④ My dad planted flowers _____ the weekend.
⑤ I practiced the piano _____ three days.

고난도
[12-13] 다음 중 밑줄 친 부분이 어법상 어색한 것을 고르시오.

12 ① There is a vase <u>next</u> the window.
② The doll is <u>on</u> the shelf.
③ Are there any cars <u>in front of</u> the building?
④ She is putting the boxes <u>under</u> the desk.
⑤ Did you find the key <u>behind</u> the lamp?

13 ① We will visit our grandmother <u>on</u> New Year's day.
② James can play games <u>before</u> dinner.
③ The weather was bad <u>during</u> the holidays.
④ John Walker invented matches <u>at</u> 1826.
⑤ She talked with her friend <u>for</u> 40 minutes.

서술형
[14-16] 우리말과 같도록 괄호 안의 말을 활용하여 문장을 완성하시오.

14 태양은 구름 뒤에 있다. (the cloud)

= The sun is _____.

15 그 축제는 목요일에 시작할 것이다. (Thursday)

= The festival will start _____.

16 그 아이는 종종 침대 아래에 숨는다. (the bed)

= The kid often hides _____.

서술형
[17-18] 우리말과 같도록 괄호 안의 말을 알맞게 배열하시오.

17 그 숲에 오래된 나무 한 그루가 있다. (the forest, in, an old tree, is)

= There _____.

18 나는 항상 점심 식사 후에 이를 닦는다. (lunch, my teeth, brush, after)

= I always _____.

Chapter 09

전치사

Hackers Grammar Smart Starter

Word Review

Chapter 09에 나온 어휘 중 잘 외워지지 않는 것은 박스에 체크하여 복습하시오.

☐ **stop**	동 멈추다	☐ **sunrise**	명 일출
☐ **bridge**	명 다리	☐ **leg**	명 다리
☐ **hill**	명 언덕	☐ **stranger**	명 낯선 사람
☐ **stand**	동 서 있다	☐ **coin**	명 동전
☐ **mirror**	명 거울	☐ **leaf**	명 (나뭇)잎
☐ **closet**	명 벽장	☐ **start**	동 시작하다
☐ **wall**	명 벽	☐ **roof**	명 지붕
☐ **take a break**	잠시 휴식을 취하다	☐ **grow up**	자라다
☐ **make trouble**	말썽을 일으키다	☐ **laptop**	명 노트북
☐ **noon**	명 정오	☐ **leave**	동 떠나다
☐ **holiday**	명 휴일	☐ **end**	동 끝나다
☐ **midnight**	명 자정	☐ **take a shower**	샤워를 하다
☐ **get up**	일어나다	☐ **shelf**	명 선반
☐ **borrow**	동 빌리다	☐ **invent**	동 발명하다
☐ **suddenly**	부 갑자기	☐ **match**	명 성냥

Check-up

영어 어휘와 알맞은 우리말 뜻을 연결하시오.

1 **borrow** ·   · ⓐ 다리
2 **noon** ·   · ⓑ 정오
3 **roof** ·   · ⓒ 지붕
4 **sunrise** ·   · ⓓ 일출
5 **leg** ·   · ⓔ 빌리다

6 **match** ·   · ⓐ 언덕
7 **make trouble** ·   · ⓑ 말썽을 일으키다
8 **hill** ·   · ⓒ 선반
9 **wall** ·   · ⓓ 성냥
10 **shelf** ·   · ⓔ 벽

정답 1 ⓔ 2 ⓑ 3 ⓒ 4 ⓓ 5 ⓐ 6 ⓓ 7 ⓑ 8 ⓐ 9 ⓔ 10 ⓒ

Chapter

10

접속사

접속사는 단어와 단어, 구와 구, 절과 절을 연결하는 말이다.

UNIT 01 | and, but, or

1 **and**(~과, 그리고)

서로 비슷한 내용을 연결한다.

Mom **and** *Dad* are busy.
Carol *ate breakfast* **and** *brushed her teeth*.
I live in Seattle, **and** *Charles lives in Chicago*.

> **TIP** and를 이용해서 세 가지를 연결할 때는 「A, B, and C」의 형태로 쓴다.
> They bought *eggs, milk,* **and** *bread*.

2 **but**(하지만, 그러나)

서로 반대되는 내용을 연결한다.

Today is *sunny* **but** *cold*.
I *went to bed early* **but** *got up late*.
Amy dances well, **but** *Beth doesn't dance well*.

3 **or**(또는, ~이거나, 아니면)

두 가지 이상의 선택 사항을 연결한다.

Do you want *water* **or** *tea*?
We can go to Jejudo *by ship* **or** *by airplane*.
Did she write the letter, **or** *did you write it*?

Smart Check 다음 빈칸에 들어갈 가장 알맞은 것을 고르시오.

1 The bag is expensive _____ pretty.
① but   ② or

2 I am a student, _____ Mr. Russell is a teacher.
① and   ② or

3 Do you like cats _____ dogs?
① but   ② or

Practice

Answers p.12

A 괄호 안에서 가장 알맞은 것을 고르시오.

1 Ants are small (or / but) strong.

2 He took a shower (and / but) dried his hair.

3 Does Lena like rice (or / but) noodles?

4 I passed the test, (but / or) Jack failed it.

5 My favorite sports are tennis (but / and) badminton.

ant 몡 개미
strong 혱 강한
dry 통 말리다
noodle 몡 국수
fail 통 떨어지다, 실패하다
favorite 혱 가장 좋아하는

B 다음 빈칸에 and, but, or 중 가장 알맞은 것을 쓰시오.

1 This soup smells good _____ tastes terrible.

2 He locked the door _____ put the key in his pocket.

3 I will be a police officer _____ a firefighter.

4 Lucas, Janet, _____ Peter live in the same town.

5 You can visit my home, _____ we can meet at the park.

6 She had enough time _____ didn't finish her homework.

lock 통 잠그다
pocket 몡 주머니
police officer 경찰관
firefighter 몡 소방관
town 몡 마을
enough 혱 충분한

C 다음 그림을 보고 빈칸에 and, but, or 중 가장 알맞은 것을 쓰시오.

1  **2**  **3**

choose 통 선택하다
beef 몡 소고기

1 You can choose chicken _____ beef.

2 Eric sang a song, _____ Sandra played the guitar.

3 I like these shoes, _____ they are too big.

Chapter 10

접속사 Hackers Grammar Smart Starter

when, before, after는 시간을 나타내는 절을, because는 이유를 나타내는 절을 이끄는 접속사이다.

1

when(~할 때)

I watch comedy movies **when** I'm sad.
You must wear a helmet **when** you ride a bike.
When James arrived, the window was open.

2

before(~하기 전에)

He checked the time **before** he left.
You have to think **before** you speak.
Before I go to school, I will meet Sophie.

3

after(~한 후에)

I drink water **after** I work out.
Teresa washed the dishes **after** she baked cookies.
After he graduated, he became a doctor.

> **TIP** 시간을 나타내는 절에서는 미래시제 대신 현재시제를 쓴다.
> I will call you *after* I (~~will come~~, **come**) back home.

4

because(~하기 때문에)

My sister cried **because** she lost her bag.
Jordan can't play basketball **because** he broke his arm.
Because it was raining, I wore a raincoat.

Smart Check 다음 빈칸에 들어갈 가장 알맞은 것을 고르시오.

1 We can't lift this box _____ it is heavy.
   ① before　　　　② because

2 I listen to music _____ I take a walk.
   ① because　　　② when

3 Henry cleans his room _____ he goes to bed.
   ① before　　　　② after

Practice

Answers p.12

A 괄호 안에서 가장 알맞은 것을 고르시오.

1 He eats ice cream (because / after) he has a meal.

2 She turned on the air conditioner (after / because) it was so hot.

3 My father was a pilot (when / because) I was a baby.

4 I will help you after I (do / will do) the laundry.

5 (After / Before) you enter the room, you must knock on the door.

> have a meal 식사하다
> turn on (전기, 기계 등을) 켜다
> air conditioner 에어컨
> pilot 명 조종사
> do the laundry 빨래를 하다
> enter 동 들어가다
> knock on the door 문을 두드리다

B 다음 그림은 Rachel의 방과 후 일과이다. 빈칸에 when, before, after 중 알맞은 것을 쓰시오.

> plastic bag 비닐봉지
> glasses 명 안경

 3:30 P.M.
 4:30 P.M.
 6:00 P.M.

1 Rachel brings a plastic bag _____ she walks her dog.

2 Rachel walks her dog _____ she goes to the library.

3 _____ Rachel studies, she wears glasses.

4 Rachel buys some snacks _____ she studies.

C 우리말과 같도록 빈칸에 알맞은 접속사를 쓰시오.

1 나는 나의 방 안에 있었을 때 이상한 소리를 들었다.

= I heard a strange sound _____ I was in my room.

2 그녀는 영화가 시작하기 전에 팝콘을 가져올 것이다.

= She will get popcorn _____ the movie starts.

3 Brian은 그 책을 읽은 후에 졸려졌다.

= _____ Brian read the book, he became sleepy.

4 그들은 그 TV 쇼가 웃겼기 때문에 많이 웃었다.

= They laughed a lot _____ the TV show was funny.

> become 동 ~(해)지다
> laugh 동 웃다
> a lot 많이

Writing Exercise

A 우리말과 같도록 괄호 안의 말을 활용하여 문장을 완성하시오.

1 그 개는 내가 가까이 갔을 때 나에게 짖어댔다. (get)

= The dog barked at me _____ close.

2 Sarah는 사실을 말했지만, 그들은 그녀를 믿지 않았다. (believe)

= Sarah told the truth, _____ her.

3 그는 저 요구르트를 먹은 후에 복통이 있었다. (eat)

= He had a stomachache _____ that yogurt.

4 그가 정직하지 않기 때문에, 나는 그를 좋아하지 않는다. (be)

= _____ honest, I don't like him.

5 너는 박물관에 들어가기 전에 너의 표를 보여줘야 한다. (enter)

= You must show your ticket _____ the museum.

6 우리는 당근, 양파, 그리고 호박을 사용할 것이다. (carrots, onions, pumpkins)

= We will use _____.

B 우리말과 같도록 괄호 안의 말을 알맞게 배열하시오.

1 나는 소설이나 만화책을 빌릴 것이다. (or, novels, borrow, comic books)

= I will _____.

2 너는 경기가 시작하기 전에 준비 운동을 해야 한다. (the game, before, begins)

= You must warm up _____.

3 그녀는 밖에서 논 후에 손을 씻었다. (she, after, played)

= She washed her hands _____ outside.

4 저 여자는 Abigail이고, 중학교에서 미술을 가르친다. (teaches, and, art, she)

= That woman is Abigail, _____ at a middle school.

5 Joe는 새 바지가 필요했기 때문에 쇼핑몰에 갔다. (needed, Joe, because, new pants)

= _____, he went to the mall.

6 그들은 소금을 원했지만, 그 종업원은 그들에게 후추를 가져다줬다. (pepper, the server, but, brought)

= They wanted salt, _____ to them.

C 다음 빈칸에 가장 알맞은 접속사를 <보기>에서 한 번씩만 골라 쓰시오.

> <보기>   and   but   or   when   because

1 Is this your bag _____ Kate's bag?

2 I got a good score on the test _____ I studied hard.

3 Emily is cute, _____ her sister is pretty.

4 _____ I saw her picture, I remembered her name.

5 That medicine tastes bitter _____ is good for health.

D 다음 그림을 보고 빈칸에 알맞은 접속사를 <보기>에서 한 번씩만 골라 쓰시오.

1

2

3

4

5

6

> <보기>   and   but   when   before   after   because

1 Matt _____ Mark planned Kelly's birthday party.

2 They went to the bakery _____ they bought a present.

3 _____ Kelly came home, they hid behind the door.

4 Kelly was surprised _____ she saw the present and the cake.

5 She was very happy _____ she liked the present.

6 It was a small party, _____ they enjoyed it.

Chapter Test

[1-2] 다음 빈칸에 들어갈 가장 알맞은 것을 고르시오.

1

I had pizza _____ pasta for dinner.

① and   ② but   ③ or
④ when   ⑤ because

2

Jerry wore a scarf _____ it was too cold.

① and   ② but   ③ or
④ because   ⑤ before

서술형

[3-5] 다음 빈칸에 가장 알맞은 접속사를 <보기>에서 한 번씩만 골라 쓰시오.

<보기>   but   or   when

3

We will go to the museum _____ the bookstore today.

4

I don't like milk, _____ I like cheese.

5

The bell rang _____ the teacher arrived.

6 다음 빈칸에 들어갈 말이 나머지 넷과 <u>다른</u> 것은?

① I was late _____ I missed the bus.
② We were surprised _____ there was a deer on the road.
③ Susan cleaned the floor _____ it was dirty.
④ William can solve the quiz _____ it is easy.
⑤ It was dark outside _____ I woke up.

고난도

[7-8] 다음 빈칸에 들어갈 말이 순서대로 짝지어진 것을 고르시오.

7

• Penguins have wings, _____ they can't fly.
• I will watch that movie _____ I like comedies.

① or – because   ② and – when
③ but – because   ④ or – when
⑤ but – before

8

• Does she live in London _____ in New York?
• Owen saw a rainbow _____ the rain stopped.

① but – after   ② or – after
③ but – before   ④ or – because
⑤ and – before

[9-10] 서술형 고난도
다음 빈칸에 공통으로 들어갈 가장 알맞은 접속사를 쓰시오.

9
- Jane doesn't eat pork, _____ she eats beef.
- Math is difficult _____ interesting.

10
- Mom boiled the water _____ she put the potatoes in the pot.
- Marie sent me a text message _____ she went to sleep.

[11-12] 다음 중 밑줄 친 부분이 문맥상 어색한 것을 고르시오.

11 ① George was angry <u>or</u> calm.
② The baby laughed <u>and</u> clapped her hands.
③ They will travel to France <u>or</u> Italy.
④ I can swim, <u>but</u> Chloe can't swim.
⑤ Jessica will visit Vietnam, Thailand, <u>and</u> Malaysia.

12 ① You can play a computer game <u>after</u> you finish your homework.
② <u>Because</u> the thief ran away, he dropped the vase.
③ <u>Before</u> Jenny left, Brian gave her a gift.
④ I need new pencils <u>because</u> my pencils are short.
⑤ My family builds a snowman <u>when</u> it snows.

[13-15] 서술형
우리말과 같도록 괄호 안의 말을 활용하여 문장을 완성하시오.

13
Jonathan은 아팠기 때문에 병원에 갔다. (be sick)

= Jonathan went to the hospital _____ _____.

14
나는 자유 시간이 있을 때 책을 읽을 것이다. (have free time)

= I will read a book _____.

15
그 아이들은 모래를 가지고 논 후에 손을 씻었다. (play with sand)

= The children washed their hands _____ _____.

16 서술형 고난도
다음 문장에서 어법상 어색한 부분을 찾아 쓰고 바르게 고쳐 쓰시오.

My sister will practice the piano before she will eat dinner.

_____ → _____

Word Review

Chapter 10에 나온 어휘 중 잘 외워지지 않는 것은 박스에 체크하여 복습하시오.

☐ expensive	형 비싼	☐ bark	동 짖다
☐ dry	동 말리다	☐ believe	동 믿다
☐ lock	동 잠그다	☐ stomachache	명 복통
☐ same	형 같은	☐ pumpkin	명 호박
☐ beef	명 소고기	☐ novel	명 소설
☐ check	동 확인하다	☐ bitter	형 쓴
☐ work out	운동하다	☐ plan	동 계획하다
☐ graduate	동 졸업하다	☐ enjoy	동 즐기다
☐ become	동 ~이 되다, ~(해)지다	☐ ring	동 울리다
☐ lose	동 잃어버리다, 지다	☐ arrive	동 도착하다
☐ lift	동 들어 올리다	☐ surprised	형 놀란
☐ enter	동 들어가다	☐ wing	명 날개
☐ knock	동 두드리다	☐ boil	동 끓이다
☐ bring	동 가져오다	☐ calm	형 차분한
☐ laugh	동 웃다	☐ clap	동 박수를 치다

Check-up

영어 어휘와 알맞은 우리말 뜻을 연결하시오.

1 calm · · ⓐ 잃어버리다, 지다
2 lose · · ⓑ 차분한
3 stomachache · · ⓒ 복통
4 novel · · ⓓ 계획하다
5 plan · · ⓔ 소설

6 boil · · ⓐ 즐기다
7 enjoy · · ⓑ 비싼
8 believe · · ⓒ 끓이다
9 bark · · ⓓ 믿다
10 expensive · · ⓔ 짖다

정답 1ⓑ 2ⓐ 3ⓒ 4ⓔ 5ⓓ 6ⓒ 7ⓐ 8ⓓ 9ⓔ 10ⓑ

Chapter

11

문장의 종류

특정한 의도를 나타내기 위해 의문문, 명령문, 감탄문 등
다양한 종류의 문장을 사용할 수 있다.

UNIT 01 | 의문사 의문문 I

1 의문사 의문문

who	what	where	when	why	how
누가, 누구를	무엇이, 무엇을	어디에(서)	언제	왜	어떻게

What is your wish?
When do you jog?

2 who(누가, 누구를)

❶ 사람에 대해 물을 때 쓰며, '누구를'이라는 의미인 경우 whom으로도 쓸 수 있다.

Who called me?
Who is your brother?
Who(m) did you see on the street?

❷ whose는 '누구의'라는 의미의 형용사로 쓰여 명사 앞에서 명사를 꾸밀 수 있다.

Whose *idea* is this?
Whose *cups* are those?

3 what(무엇이, 무엇을)

❶ 동물이나 사물, 또는 사람의 직업이나 성격에 대해 물을 때 쓴다.

What is on the table?
What do you want for dinner?
What does his mother do?

❷ '무슨, 어떤'이라는 의미의 형용사로 쓰여 명사 앞에서 명사를 꾸밀 수 있다.

What *day* is it today?
What *subject* do you like?

Smart Check 다음 빈칸에 들어갈 알맞은 것을 고르시오.

1 _____ is that boy?
① Who   ② Whom

2 _____ movie did you watch yesterday?
① Who   ② What

3 _____ is your dream?
① Whom   ② What

4 _____ bags are these?
① Whose   ② Who

Practice

A 괄호 안에서 알맞은 것을 고르시오.

1 (Who / What) is her best friend?

2 (Who / What) color does he like?

3 (Whose / Who) pen is this?

4 (Who / Whom) stole my wallet?

5 (Who / What) is Janet's hobby?

6 (Whom / What) did you buy at the supermarket?

7 (Whom / Whose) did you meet last weekend?

color 명 색깔
steal 동 훔치다
wallet 명 지갑
hobby 명 취미

B 다음 질문에 대한 대답을 <보기>에서 골라 그 기호를 쓰시오.

> <보기>
> ⓐ I chatted with Judy.
> ⓑ They are Tim's earphones.
> ⓒ He borrowed *The Giver*.
> ⓓ My brother is in the playground.

1 *A*: Who is in the playground?　　*B*: _____

2 *A*: Whom did you chat with last night?　　*B*: _____

3 *A*: Whose earphones are these?　　*B*: _____

4 *A*: What book did Greg borrow?　　*B*: _____

chat 동 수다를 떨다
earphone 명 이어폰
borrow 동 빌리다
playground 명 놀이터, 운동장

C 다음 대화의 빈칸에 알맞은 말을 <보기>에서 골라 쓰시오.

> <보기>　　who　　whose　　what

1 *A*: _____ washed the dishes last night?
　 B: Dad washed the dishes.

2 *A*: _____ is she wearing now?
　 B: She is wearing jeans.

3 *A*: _____ shoes are these?
　 B: They are my shoes.

4 *A*: _____ did you invite to the party?
　 B: I invited my classmates.

jeans 명 (청)바지

UNIT 02 | 의문사 의문문 II

1 **where**(어디에(서))

장소를 물을 때 쓴다.

Where is the park?　　　　　　**Where** did he find the key?

---

2 **when**(언제)

시간이나 날짜를 물을 때 쓰며, 시간을 물을 때는 what time으로 바꿔 쓸 수 있다.

When(= **What time**) does the TV show start?
When is Children's Day?

---

3 **why**(왜)

이유를 물을 때 쓰며, because(왜냐하면)를 사용하여 대답할 수 있다.

A: **Why** do you like flowers?
B: *Because* they are pretty.

---

4 **how**(어떻게)

방법이나 상태를 물을 때 쓴다.

How did she make pasta?　　　　　**How** was your vacation?

---

5 **how + 형용사/부사**(얼마나 ~한/하게)

높이, 길이, 거리, 나이 등의 구체적인 정보를 물을 때 쓴다.

How tall is the tower? <높이, 키>　　　　**How long** is the Hangang? <길이, 기간>
How far is your school? <거리>　　　　　**How old** is your sister? <나이>
How many pens does he have? <개수>　　**How much** is that computer? <가격, 양>
How often do you listen to music? <빈도>

Smart Check　다음 빈칸에 들어갈 알맞은 것을 고르시오.

1 *A*: _____ will we meet?
　　B: At 5 P.M.
　　① When　　　　② How

2 *A*: _____ do you study English?
　　B: I read English books.
　　① Where　　　② How

3 *A*: _____ does Miranda live?
　　B: She lives in Paris.
　　① Where　　　② Why

4 *A*: _____ did he cry?
　　B: Because he lost his phone.
　　① When　　　② Why

Practice

Answers p.13

A 괄호 안에서 알맞은 것을 고르시오.

1 A: (Where / When) does Ms. Wilson work?

   B: She works at a hospital.

2 A: (Where / Why) was he upset?

   B: Because he failed the test.

3 A: (How / Why) was the camping trip?

   B: It was fun.

4 A: (How / When) does the train arrive?

   B: It arrives at 10:15.

5 A: How (long / much) is that bridge?

   B: It is 500 meters long.

hospital 몡 병원
upset 혱 속상한
bridge 몡 다리

B 다음 질문에 대한 대답을 <보기>에서 골라 그 기호를 쓰시오.

<보기>	ⓐ It rings at 8 A.M.
	ⓑ I will visit them next weekend.
	ⓒ You can take a shuttle bus.
	ⓓ Because I am going to make jam.

1 A: Why did you buy strawberries?   B: _____

2 A: How can I go to the theme park?   B: _____

3 A: What time does your alarm clock ring?   B: _____

4 A: When will you visit your grandparents?   B: _____

ring 동 울리다
shuttle bus 셔틀버스
alarm clock 자명종

C 다음 대화의 빈칸에 알맞은 말을 <보기>에서 골라 쓰시오.

<보기>	how tall	how old	how many	how often

1 A: _____ do you eat fast food?

   B: Once a month.

2 A: _____ is your brother?

   B: He is 180 centimeters.

3 A: _____ students are in the classroom?

   B: There are 25 students.

4 A: _____ is that pine tree?

   B: It is about 100 years old.

fast food 패스트푸드
pine tree 소나무

UNIT 03 | 명령문, 청유문, 감탄문

1 명령문

상대방에게 지시하거나 요구하는 문장이며, 주어 You가 생략되어 있다.

긍정 명령문(~해라)	동사원형
부정 명령문(~하지 마라)	Don't[Do not] + 동사원형

Wash your hands.
Don't[Do not] eat too much.

> **TIP** 명령문 맨 앞이나 맨 뒤에 please를 붙이면 더 정중한 표현이 된다.
> **Please** *open* the window. (= *Open* the window, **please**.)

2 청유문

상대방에게 권유하거나 제안하는 문장이다.

긍정 청유문((우리) ~하자)	Let's + 동사원형
부정 청유문((우리) ~하지 말자)	Let's not + 동사원형

Let's play outside.
Let's not be late for school.

3 감탄문

기쁨이나 놀라움 등의 감정을 나타내는 문장으로, '정말 ~이구나/하구나!'의 의미이다. 문장 맨 뒤의 「주어 + 동사」는 생략할 수도 있다.

What 감탄문(명사 강조)	What + (a/an) + 형용사 + 명사 + (주어 + 동사)!
How 감탄문(형용사나 부사 강조)	How + 형용사/부사 + (주어 + 동사)!

What a sad movie *(this is)*!
How pretty *(the baby is)*!
How kindly *he speaks*!
→ How 감탄문이 부사를 강조할 때는 문장 맨 뒤의 「주어 + 동사」를 생략할 수 없다.

> **TIP** What 감탄문이 복수명사나 셀 수 없는 명사를 강조할 때는 **a/an**을 쓰지 않는다.
> **What old pictures** (these are)!
> **What delicious bread** (it is)!

Smart Check 다음 빈칸에 들어갈 알맞은 것을 고르시오.

1 _____ your room now.
  ① Clean   ② Cleaning

2 _____ a funny joke it is!
  ① How   ② What

Practice

Answers p.13

A 괄호 안에서 알맞은 것을 고르시오.

1 (What / How) a great song it is!

2 (Turn / Turns) on the light, please.

3 (What / How) cute your brother is!

4 (Don't / Doesn't) sit on the floor.

5 (Lets / Let's) take some pictures.

6 What exciting books (are those / those are)!

turn on the light 불을 켜다
floor 형 바닥
take a picture 사진을 찍다
exciting 형 흥미진진한

B 우리말과 같도록 괄호 안의 동사를 활용하여 빈칸에 쓰시오.

1 큰 소리로 말하지 마라. (talk) = _____ _____ loudly.

2 길을 건너자. (cross) = _____ _____ the street.

3 방과 후에 나에게 전화해라. (call) = _____ me after school.

4 시간을 낭비하지 말자. (waste) = _____ _____ _____ time.

5 너의 친구를 도와줘라. (help) = _____ your friend.

cross the street 길을 건너다
call 통 전화하다, 부르다
waste 통 낭비하다

C 다음 그림을 보고 괄호 안의 말을 활용하여 감탄문을 완성하시오.

brave 형 용감한

1  2  3

1 _____ they are! (nice cars)

2 _____ Richard jumps! (high)

3 _____ she is! (brave)

Writing Exercise

A 우리말과 같도록 <보기>의 말을 활용하여 문장을 완성하시오.

<보기>	who	what	where	when

1 그 가게는 언제 문을 닫니? = _____ does the store close?

2 너는 어디에서 저녁을 먹었니? = _____ did you have dinner?

3 누가 답을 아니? = _____ knows the answer?

4 그녀가 가장 좋아하는 영화는 무엇이니? = _____ is her favorite movie?

<보기>	lie	enter	take	wait

5 안에서 기다리자. = _____ inside.

6 이 우산을 가지고 가라. = _____ this umbrella.

7 나에게 거짓말하지 마라. = _____ to me.

8 이 건물에 들어가지 말자. = _____ this building.

B 우리말과 같도록 괄호 안의 말을 활용하여 문장을 완성하시오.

1 하늘이 정말 맑구나! (clear)

= _____ the sky is!

2 빠르게 먹지 말자. (eat)

= _____ fast.

3 Tyler는 정말 똑똑한 소년이구나! (a smart boy)

= _____ Tyler is!

4 너의 부모님께 공손해라. (be, polite)

= _____ to your parents.

5 이것들은 누구의 양말이니? (socks)

= _____ are these?

6 얼마나 많은 방문객들이 줄을 서서 기다리고 있니? (visitors)

= _____ are waiting in line?

C 다음 빈칸에 알맞은 말을 넣어 대화를 완성하시오.

1 A: _____ is that river?

B: About 20 kilometers long.

2 A: _____ size do you want?

B: I want the small size.

3 A: _____ rode my bicycle?

B: Tom rode it.

4 A: _____ are you going now?

B: I'm going to the library.

5 A: _____ does James hate winter?

B: Because he doesn't like cold weather.

6 A: _____ did Emma leave Seoul?

B: She left Seoul three weeks ago.

7 A: _____ is your cat?

B: It is seven months old.

D 다음 그림을 보고 <보기>의 말을 활용하여 명령문이나 감탄문을 완성하시오.

1    **2**    **3**    **4**

<보기>	eat	feed	strongly	a huge waterfall

1 _____ the birds.

2 _____ it is!

3 _____ more vegetables.

4 _____ the wind blows!

Chapter Test

[1-2] 다음 빈칸에 들어갈 알맞은 것을 고르시오.

1

| _____ go on a picnic today. |

① Be   ② Let   ③ Let's
④ Not   ⑤ What

2

| _____ beautiful the dress is! |

① Who   ② When   ③ What
④ How   ⑤ Why

서술형

[3-5] 다음 빈칸에 알맞은 의문사를 넣어 대화를 완성하시오.

3

A: _____ jacket is this?
B: It's Kate's jacket.

4

A: _____ is your plan for the summer vacation?
B: I am going to learn tennis.

5

A: _____ do you like that writer?
B: Because her books are interesting.

[6-7] 다음 중 어법상 <u>어색한</u> 것을 고르시오.

6
① Water the plants, please.
② Don't be nervous.
③ Let's have ice cream for dessert.
④ Take your water bottle before you leave.
⑤ Let's watch not the news program.

7
① How colorful the leaves are!
② What a fast computer it is!
③ What boring movies they are!
④ How an old the car is!
⑤ What delicious soup this is!

8 다음 대화의 빈칸에 공통으로 들어갈 알맞은 것은?

A: _____ is that animal in the picture?
B: It's my lizard.
A: _____ a small lizard it is!

① Who   ② What   ③ Where
④ Why   ⑤ How

서술형

9 다음 대화에서 어법상 <u>어색한</u> 부분을 찾아 쓰고 바르게 고쳐 쓰시오.

A: Why can I go to the mall?
B: Take the subway Line 2.

_____ → _____

10 다음 중 자연스럽지 <u>않은</u> 대화는?

① A: How many people did you invite?
　B: I invited eight people.

② A: Where did you buy the postcard?
　B: I bought it yesterday.

③ A: Who was in the classroom?
　B: Sarah was there.

④ A: What time did you come home?
　B: At 6 o'clock.

⑤ A: What did Tom cook?
　B: He cooked hot dogs.

고난도

11 다음 대화의 빈칸에 들어갈 말이 순서대로 짝지어진 것은?

> A: _____ is your room so cold?
> B: Because Maria broke the window.
> 　_____ turn on the heater.

① Why – Let's 　　② What – Don't
③ What – Let's 　　④ Why – Don't
⑤ Why – Let's not

서술형

[12-13] 우리말과 같도록 괄호 안의 말을 알맞게 배열하시오.

12
> 우리는 얼마나 오래 기다렸니? (wait, long, we, did, how)

= _____ ?

13
> 이것은 정말 깨끗한 방이구나! (room, is, a, this, what, clean)

= _____ !

서술형 고난도

[14-17] 우리말과 같도록 괄호 안의 말을 활용하여 문장을 완성하시오.

14
> 그들은 내일 누구를 만날 거니? (meet)

= _____ tomorrow?

15
> 너는 이 모자를 어디에서 샀니? (buy this hat)

= _____ ?

16
> 저 식당에서 피자를 주문하지 말자. (order pizza)

= _____ from that restaurant.

17
> 미술관에서 사진을 찍지 마라. (take pictures)

= _____ in the gallery.

Word Review

Chapter 11에 나온 어휘 중 잘 외워지지 않는 것은 박스에 체크하여 복습하시오.

□ idea	몡 생각	□ answer	몡 답; 통 답하다
□ subject	몡 과목	□ lie	통 거짓말하다
□ dream	몡 꿈; 통 꿈꾸다	□ clear	형 맑은, 깨끗한
□ steal	통 훔치다	□ polite	형 예의 바른, 공손한
□ chat	통 수다를 떨다	□ sock	몡 양말
□ jeans	몡 (청)바지	□ hate	통 싫어하다
□ work	통 일하다	□ weather	몡 날씨
□ upset	형 속상한	□ huge	형 막대한, 거대한
□ visit	통 방문하다	□ waterfall	몡 폭포
□ pine tree	소나무	□ blow	통 불다
□ light	몡 불, 빛	□ picnic	몡 소풍
□ call	통 전화하다, 부르다	□ beautiful	형 아름다운
□ waste	통 낭비하다	□ boring	형 지루한
□ help	통 돕다	□ lizard	몡 도마뱀
□ brave	형 용감한	□ invite	통 초대하다

Check-up

영어 어휘와 알맞은 우리말 뜻을 연결하시오.

1 waste ·   · ⓐ 낭비하다

2 blow ·   · ⓑ 불다

3 lizard ·   · ⓒ 지루한

4 boring ·   · ⓓ 도마뱀

5 steal ·   · ⓔ 훔치다

6 invite ·   · ⓐ 아름다운

7 polite ·   · ⓑ 속상한

8 upset ·   · ⓒ 예의 바른, 공손한

9 brave ·   · ⓓ 용감한

10 beautiful ·   · ⓔ 초대하다

정답 1ⓐ 2ⓑ 3ⓓ 4ⓒ 5ⓔ 6ⓔ 7ⓒ 8ⓑ 9ⓓ 10ⓐ

불규칙 동사 변화표

1. A-A-A형 원형-과거형-과거분사형이 모두 같은 경우

원형	과거형	과거분사형
cost 비용이 들다	cost	cost
hit 치다, 때리다	hit	hit
hurt 다치게 하다	hurt	hurt
let ~하게 하다	let	let

원형	과거형	과거분사형
put 놓다	put	put
read[ri:d] 읽다	read[red]	read[red]
shut 닫다	shut	shut
spread 펼치다	spread	spread

2. A-B-A형 원형-과거분사형이 같은 경우

원형	과거형	과거분사형
become ~이 되다	became	become
come 오다	came	come

원형	과거형	과거분사형
overcome 극복하다	overcame	overcome
run 달리다	ran	run

3. A-B-B형 과거형-과거분사형이 같은 경우

원형	과거형	과거분사형
bring 가져오다	brought	brought
build 짓다, 만들다	built	built
feed 먹이를 주다	fed	fed
feel 느끼다	felt	felt
find 찾다	found	found
get 얻다	got	got(ten)
have 가지다	had	had
hear 듣다	heard	heard
keep 유지하다	kept	kept
lay 놓다, 낳다	laid	laid
lead 이끌다	led	led

원형	과거형	과거분사형
leave 떠나다	left	left
lose 잃다, 지다	lost	lost
make 만들다	made	made
meet 만나다	met	met
send 보내다	sent	sent
sleep 자다	slept	slept
spend 쓰다	spent	spent
tell 말하다	told	told
think 생각하다	thought	thought
understand 이해하다	understood	understood
win 이기다	won	won

4. A-B-C형 원형-과거형-과거분사형이 모두 다른 경우

원형	과거형	과거분사형	원형	과거형	과거분사형
be ~이다, ~하다	was/were	been	hide 숨다	hid	hidden
bear 낳다	bore	born	know 알다	knew	known
begin 시작하다	began	begun	lie 눕다	lay	lain
bite 물다	bit	bitten	mistake 실수하다	mistook	mistaken
blow 불다	blew	blown	ride 타다	rode	ridden
break 깨다	broke	broken	ring 울리다	rang	rung
choose 선택하다	chose	chosen	rise 오르다	rose	risen
do 하다	did	done	see 보다	saw	seen
draw 그리다	drew	drawn	shake 흔들다	shook	shaken
drink 마시다	drank	drunk	show 보여주다	showed	showed shown
drive 운전하다	drove	driven	sing 노래하다	sang	sung
eat 먹다	ate	eaten	sink 가라앉다	sank	sunk sunken
fall 떨어지다, 넘어지다	fell	fallen	sow (씨를) 뿌리다	sowed	sowed sown
fly 날다	flew	flown	speak 말하다	spoke	spoken
forbid 금지하다	forbade	forbidden	steal 훔치다	stole	stolen
forget 잊다	forgot	forgotten	swell 붓다, 부풀다	swelled	swelled swollen
forgive 용서하다	forgave	forgiven	swim 수영하다	swam	swum
freeze 얼다	froze	frozen	take 가지고 가다	took	taken
give 주다	gave	given	throw 던지다	threw	thrown
go 가다	went	gone	wear 입고 있다	wore	worn
grow 자라다	grew	grown	write 쓰다	wrote	written

문법 사항	세부 내용	Starter	Level 1	Level 2	Level 3
be동사	be동사	p.32, 34, 36	O		
	There + be동사	p.38	O		
일반동사	일반동사	p.46, 48, 50, 52	O		
시제	현재시제	p.32, 46	O	O	
	과거시제	p.36, 50	O	O	
	미래시제	p.72	O	O	
	현재진행시제	p.70	O	O	
	과거진행시제		O	O	
	현재완료시제			O	O
	과거완료시제				O
	미래완료시제				O
조동사	can	p.80	O	O	O
	may	p.80	O	O	O
	will	p.72	O	O	
	must	p.82	O	O	O
	have to	p.82	O	O	O
	should		O	O	O
	would like to			O	
	had better			O	O
	used to			O	O
	would rather				O
	may as well				O
	조동사 + have + p.p.				O
수동태	수동태			O	O
	수동태의 다양한 형태			O	O
	4형식/5형식 문장의 수동태			O	O
	by 이외의 전치사를 쓰는 수동태			O	O
	목적어가 that절인 문장의 수동태				O
	구동사의 수동태				O
부정사	to부정사		O	O	O
	부정사를 목적격 보어로 쓰는 동사		O		O
	to부정사의 의미상 주어			O	O
	to부정사의 시제, 태				O
	to부정사 구문		O	O	O
	독립 부정사				O
동명사	동명사		O	O	O
분사	현재분사, 과거분사			O	O
	분사구문			O	O
	주의해야 할 분사구문				O
동사의 종류	주격 보어가 필요한 동사		O		
	감각동사	p.90	O	O	
	두 개의 목적어가 필요한 동사(수여동사)	p.92	O	O	
	목적격 보어가 필요한 동사		O	O	

문법 사항	세부 내용	Starter	Level 1	Level 2	Level 3
문장의 종류	명령문, 청유문, 감탄문	p.124	O		
	의문사 의문문	p.120, 122	O		
	부정의문문, 선택의문문, 부가의문문		O		
명사와 관사	셀 수 있는 명사, 셀 수 없는 명사	p.12, 14	O		
	관사		O		
대명사	인칭대명사	p.22	O		
	재귀대명사		O	O	
	지시대명사	p.24	O		
	비인칭 주어 it	p.24	O		
	부정대명사		O	O	
형용사와 부사	형용사, 부사	p.60, 62	O		
비교구문	원급/비교급/최상급 비교		O	O	O
	비교구문을 이용한 표현			O	O
전치사	장소 전치사	p.100	O		
	시간 전치사	p.102	O		
	기타 전치사		O		
접속사	등위접속사	p.110	O		
	시간 접속사	p.112	O	O	O
	이유 접속사	p.112	O	O	O
	결과 접속사			O	O
	조건 접속사		O	O	O
	양보 접속사			O	O
	that		O	O	
	명령문 + and/or		O	O	
	상관접속사		O	O	O
	간접의문문				O
관계사	관계대명사			O	O
	관계부사			O	O
	주의해야 할 관계사의 쓰임			O	O
	관계사의 계속적 용법				O
	복합관계사				O
가정법	가정법 과거, 가정법 과거완료			O	O
	혼합 가정법				O
	I wish 가정법			O	O
	as if 가정법			O	O
	It's time 가정법				O
	Without[But for] 가정법				O
	if를 생략한 가정법				O
일치와 화법	시제의 일치			O	O
	수의 일치				O
	화법			O	O
특수구문	강조, 도치, 병렬, 부정, 동격, 생략				O

MEMO

Smart, Useful, and Essential Grammar

HACKERS
GRAMMAR
SMART
STARTER

초판 4쇄 발행 2024년 3월 4일
초판 1쇄 발행 2022년 1월 3일

지은이	해커스 어학연구소
펴낸곳	㈜해커스 어학연구소
펴낸이	해커스 어학연구소 출판팀

주소	서울특별시 서초구 강남대로61길 23 ㈜해커스 어학연구소
고객센터	02-537-5000
교재 관련 문의	publishing@hackers.com
	해커스북 사이트(HackersBook.com) 고객센터 Q&A 게시판
동영상강의	star.Hackers.com

ISBN	978-89-6542-454-3 (53740)
Serial Number	01-04-01

중고등영어 1위,
해커스북 HackersBook.com

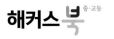

· 깊은 이해로 이끄는 **예문/문제 해석**
· 불규칙 동사의 확실한 암기를 돕는 **불규칙 동사 테스트**
· 학습한 단어의 암기 여부를 쉽게 점검할 수 있는 **단어 리스트 및 단어 테스트**
· 교재의 단어를 언제 어디서나 들으면서 외우는 **단어암기 MP3**
· 서술형 시험을 완벽하게 대비할 수 있는 **영작/해석 워크시트**

한경비즈니스 선정 2020 한국품질만족도 교육(온·오프라인 중·고등영어) 부문 1위

HACKERS

GRAMMAR
SMART STARTER

WORKBOOK

HACKERS
GRAMMAR
SMART STARTER

WORKBOOK

Answers p.15

UNIT 01 셀 수 있는 명사

A 괄호 안에서 알맞은 것을 고르시오.

1 Helen is (a / an) singer.

2 Four (pig / pigs) are on the farm.

3 I have two (photos / photoes).

4 Red (leafs / leaves) are on the road.

5 There are six (deer / deers) in the forest.

B a 또는 an과 괄호 안의 명사를 활용하여 문장을 완성하시오.

1 She has _____. (idea)

2 Robert wants _____. (watch)

3 _____ has a long nose. (elephant)

4 Mr. Hall is _____. (scientist)

5 There is _____ in this town. (university)

C 괄호 안의 말을 활용하여 문장을 완성하시오.

1 This is _____. (a/an, carrot)

2 Kate needs _____ in her room. (two, chair)

3 He brings _____ every day. (a/an, umbrella)

4 There are _____ on the street. (five, bus)

5 The baby has _____. (four, tooth)

D 우리말과 같도록 괄호 안의 명사를 활용하여 문장을 완성하시오.

1 나의 여동생은 매일 사과 한 개를 먹는다. (apple)
= My sister eats _____ every day.

2 부엌에 남자 세 명이 있다. (man)
= There are _____ in the kitchen.

3 나는 화요일에 수업 다섯 개를 듣는다. (class)
= I take _____ on Tuesday.

4 그들은 장난감 일곱 개를 가지고 있다. (toy)
= They have _____.

UNIT 02 셀 수 없는 명사

A 다음 빈칸에 a와 an 중 알맞은 것을 쓰고, 필요하지 않으면 X를 쓰시오.

1 I write _____ e-mail.

2 He studies with _____ Marco.

3 There is _____ jam in the jar.

4 She plays with _____ cat.

5 This magazine is about _____ health.

B 괄호 안에서 알맞은 것을 고르시오.

1 I want two (soup / bowls of soup).

2 His uncle lives in (California / a California).

3 She needs (help / helps) with her homework.

4 There are three (piece / pieces) of cheese on the dish.

5 Bobby orders four cups of (coffee / coffees) every morning.

C 다음 문장의 밑줄 친 부분을 바르게 고쳐 쓰시오.

1 The cook uses salts every day. → _____

2 They have three slice of cake for dessert. → _____

3 An Amy comes home early on Wednesdays. → _____

4 He drinks two glasses of milks in the afternoon. → _____

D 우리말과 같도록 괄호 안의 명사를 활용하여 문장을 완성하시오.

1 Alice는 물 두 병을 가지고 있다. (water)

= Alice has _____.

2 제주도는 아름다운 섬이다. (Jejudo)

= _____ is a beautiful island.

3 그는 종이 열 장이 필요하다. (paper)

= He needs _____.

4 Harris씨는 그녀의 아이들을 위해 행복을 원한다. (happiness)

= Ms. Harris wants _____ for her children.

A a 또는 an과 괄호 안의 말을 활용하여 문장을 완성하시오. (단, a나 an이 필요하지 않으면 쓰지 마시오.)

1 He needs _____ now. (air)

2 Jake wears _____. (uniform)

3 We always talk about _____. (kindness)

4 They eat _____ in the morning. (orange)

5 Mom makes _____ on Sundays. (apple pie)

6 Ms. Jones goes to _____ every year. (Europe)

7 I have _____. (blue umbrella)

B 우리말과 같도록 <보기>의 명사를 활용하여 영작하시오.

<보기>	tea	bus	story	child

1 버스 세 대 = _____

2 아이 일곱 명 = _____

3 차 다섯 잔 = _____

4 이야기 네 개 = _____

<보기>	soup	man	watch	fish

5 수프 네 그릇 = _____

6 시계 여섯 개 = _____

7 물고기 두 마리 = _____

8 남자 열 명 = _____

C 우리말과 같도록 괄호 안의 명사를 활용하여 문장을 완성하시오.

1 그의 팀은 희망을 가지고 있다. (hope)

= His team has _____.

2 펭귄은 두 발로 걷는다. (foot)

= A penguin walks with _____.

3 나의 주머니 안에 돈이 있다. (money)

= There is _____ in my pocket.

4 그녀는 그녀의 햄버거에 치즈를 원한다. (cheese)

= She wants _____ on her hamburger.

5 언덕 위에 초등학교 하나가 있다. (elementary school)

= There is _____ on the hill.

6 Eric은 밤에 우유 한 잔을 마신다. (milk)

= Eric drinks _____ at night.

D 우리말과 같도록 괄호 안의 말을 알맞게 배열하시오.

1 Olivia는 매주 초콜릿 쿠키를 만든다. (chocolate cookies, makes)

= Olivia _____ every week.

2 나의 형은 피자 다섯 조각을 먹는다. (pizza, five, of, pieces, eats)

= My brother _____.

3 자유의 여신상은 뉴욕에 있다. (is, New York, in)

= The Statue of Liberty _____.

4 그들은 금요일마다 영화 한 편을 본다. (a, watch, movie)

= They _____ on Fridays.

5 그녀는 샌드위치를 위해 빵 두 조각이 필요하다. (two, of, needs, bread, slices)

= She _____ for a sandwich.

6 Foster씨는 매일 물 네 병을 마신다. (bottles, water, drinks, four, of)

= Mr. Foster _____ every day.

A 괄호 안에서 알맞은 것을 고르시오.

1 I like (it / its) color.

2 The quiz is easy for (I / me).

3 We need (you / your) help.

4 (They / Their) play soccer after school.

B 다음 문장의 밑줄 친 부분을 알맞은 인칭대명사로 바꿔 쓰시오.

1 This is David's e-mail address.   → _____

2 Her sister is five years old.   → _____

3 He invites Laura and me every Saturday. → _____

4 We take pictures of the flowers.   → _____

C 괄호 안의 말을 활용하여 빈칸에 알맞은 말을 쓰시오.

1 This is _____ camera. (I)

2 Her parents worry about _____. (she)

3 I have _____ pens. (Kevin)

4 _____ vacation is very long. (we)

5 My brother remembers _____. (you)

D 우리말과 같도록 빈칸에 알맞은 말을 쓰시오.

1 이것은 그녀의 필통이다.   = This is _____ pencil case.

2 그 선생님은 그들에 대해 이야기한다.   = The teacher talks about _____.

3 너의 모자는 거실에 있다.   = _____ hat is in the living room.

4 그 개는 매일 우리에게 짖어댄다.   = The dog barks at _____ every day.

5 나는 때때로 Mark의 교실에 간다.   = I sometimes go to _____ classroom.

A　괄호 안에서 알맞은 것을 고르시오.

1　(That / Those) are old sneakers.

2　(That / It) is winter in Korea.

3　My mother works at (that / those) store.

4　He likes (this / these) movie characters.

B　다음 빈칸에 알맞은 말을 <보기>에서 골라 쓰시오.

<보기>　　this　　　these　　　it

1　_____ is bright in here.

2　_____ singers are very popular.

3　_____ is my homeroom teacher.

<보기>　　that　　　those　　　it

4　_____ are his gloves.

5　_____ is February 14 today.

6　_____ woman is a doctor.

C　우리말과 같도록 괄호 안의 말을 활용하여 문장을 완성하시오.

1　저 건물들은 높다. (buildings)　　= _____ are tall.

2　이 티셔츠는 나에게 크다. (T-shirt)　　= _____ is big for me.

3　이 바나나들은 신선하다. (bananas)　　= _____ are fresh.

D　우리말과 같도록 괄호 안의 말을 알맞게 배열하시오.

1　이 사람들은 나의 가족 구성원들이다. (are, family members, these, my)

　　= _____ .

2　Terry는 저 아파트에 산다. (apartment, Terry, that, lives in)

　　= _____ .

3　쇼핑몰까지 100미터이다. (it, 100 meters, is)

　　= _____ to the shopping mall.

Writing Exercise ✚

Answers p.15

A 다음 문장의 밑줄 친 부분을 알맞은 인칭대명사로 바꿔 빈칸에 쓰시오. (단, 인칭대명사의 격에 주의하시오.)

1 This is my dog. _____ has short hair.

2 Noah likes his friends. He trusts _____.

3 I have a gift for Chris. Today is _____ birthday.

4 My aunt is a cook. _____ pasta is delicious.

5 Mr. Walter has a daughter. He is proud of _____.

6 Jessica and I are on the same team. _____ are good players.

B 우리말과 같도록 빈칸에 알맞은 말을 쓰시오.

1 나는 너의 조언을 원한다. = I want _____ advice.

2 여름에는 덥다. = _____ is hot in summer.

3 그들은 용감한 군인들이다. = _____ are brave soldiers.

4 이 시험은 정말 어렵다. = _____ test is so difficult.

5 이 돌고래들은 영리하다. = _____ dolphins are clever.

6 Helen은 나와 함께 배드민턴을 친다. = Helen plays badminton with _____.

7 저 남자는 매일 안경을 쓴다. = _____ man wears glasses every day.

8 그의 삼촌은 경찰관이시다. = _____ uncle is a police officer.

C 우리말과 같도록 괄호 안의 말을 활용하여 빈칸에 쓰시오.

1 그녀는 그들의 계획을 알고 있다. (plan)

= She knows _____ _____ .

2 오늘은 월요일이다. (Monday)

= _____ _____ _____ today.

3 나의 눈은 갈색이다. (eyes)

= _____ _____ are brown.

4 저 소들은 풀을 먹는다. (cows)

= _____ _____ eat grass.

5 이것들은 수학 교과서이다. (math textbooks)

= _____ _____ _____ _____ .

6 저것은 새 도서관이다. (a new library)

= _____ _____ _____ _____ _____ .

D 우리말과 같도록 괄호 안의 말을 알맞게 배열하시오.

1 이것은 나의 독후감이다. (book report, is, this, my)

= _____ .

2 그의 엄마는 오후 5시에 저녁 식사를 만드신다. (dinner, his, makes, mom)

= _____ at 5 P.M.

3 저 기차는 공항으로 간다. (goes to, that, the airport, train)

= _____ .

4 우리의 부모님은 매일 우리에 대해 생각하신다. (think about, parents, us, our)

= _____ every day.

5 저 새끼 고양이들은 아침에 우유를 마신다. (kittens, milk, those, drink)

= _____ in the morning.

6 버스 정류장까지 2킬로미터이다. (two kilometers, is, it)

= _____ to the bus stop.

UNIT 01　be동사의 현재형

Answers p.16

A　괄호 안에서 알맞은 것을 고르시오.

1　He (am / is) my uncle.

2　I (am / is) excited now.

3　Giraffes (is / are) very tall.

4　Your sister (is / are) in the kitchen.

5　Sarah and I (am / are) 14 years old.

B　다음 빈칸에 알맞은 be동사의 현재형을 쓰시오.

1　She _____ a good swimmer.

2　I _____ proud of my parents.

3　Mr. Davis _____ from Sweden.

4　Those dogs _____ active.

5　You and Sophie _____ close friends.

C　다음 문장의 밑줄 친 부분을 줄여 완전한 문장을 쓰시오.

1　<u>They are</u> my classmates.　→ _____.

2　<u>We are</u> at the flower shop.　→ _____.

3　<u>I am</u> tired today.　→ _____.

4　<u>She is</u> on the boat.　→ _____.

5　<u>It is</u> Emily's laptop.　→ _____.

D　우리말과 같도록 괄호 안의 말과 be동사를 활용하여 문장을 완성하시오.

1　그들의 이야기는 매우 흥미롭다. (their stories)

= _____ very interesting.

2　Kelly는 시장에 있다. (Kelly)

= _____ in the market.

3　우리는 어두운 곳을 무서워한다. (we)

= _____ afraid of dark places.

4　그 남자는 주인공이다. (the man)

= _____ the main character.

UNIT 02　be동사 현재형의 부정문과 의문문

A　괄호 안에서 알맞은 것을 고르시오.

1　They (isn't / aren't) at the café.

2　(Are / Is) John and Dave Americans?

3　My name (isn't / aren't) Doris.

4　A: Are you an actor?
　　　B: Yes, (you are / I am).

B　다음 문장을 부정문으로 바꿔 쓰시오. (단, 줄임말로 쓰시오.)

1　He is my favorite artist.　　→ _____ my favorite artist.

2　This question is difficult.　　→ _____ difficult.

3　I am a big fan of baseball.　　→ _____ a big fan of baseball.

4　Chris and I are on the bus.　　→ _____ on the bus.

C　괄호 안의 말과 be동사의 현재형을 활용하여 대화를 완성하시오.

1　A: _____ a famous city? (New York)
　　　B: Yes, _____.

2　A: _____ good at soccer? (Samuel)
　　　B: No, _____.

3　A: _____ close? (you and your brother)
　　　B: Yes, _____.

D　우리말과 같도록 괄호 안의 말과 be동사를 활용하여 문장을 완성하시오. (단, 부정문에서는 줄임말을 쓰시오.)

1　Wilson씨는 바이올린 연주자가 아니다. (Mr. Wilson)
　　　= _____ a violinist.

2　저 소년들은 나의 사촌이 아니다. (those boys)
　　　= _____ my cousins.

3　이 오렌지들은 신선하니? (these oranges)
　　　= _____ fresh?

4　그 목도리는 옷장 안에 있니? (the scarf)
　　　= _____ in the closet?

UNIT 03 be동사의 과거형

A 괄호 안에서 알맞은 것을 고르시오.

1 Roy and I (was / were) in Jejudo last summer.

2 She (was / is) a fashion model three years ago.

3 The weather (isn't / wasn't) warm yesterday.

4 A: (Was / Were) the students late for class yesterday?
   B: No, they (were / weren't).

B 다음 문장을 부정문으로 바꿔 쓰시오. (단, 줄임말로 쓰시오.)

1 Alex was at the hotel last night. → _____ at the hotel last night.

2 These pictures were expensive. → _____ expensive.

3 They were in the same team. → _____ in the same team.

4 The sunlight was strong yesterday. → _____ strong yesterday.

C 괄호 안의 말과 be동사의 과거형을 활용하여 대화를 완성하시오.

1 A: _____ boring? (the musical)
   B: No, _____.

2 A: _____ popular? (these singers)
   B: No, _____.

3 A: _____ at the airport yesterday? (George)
   B: Yes, _____.

D 우리말과 같도록 괄호 안의 말과 be동사를 활용하여 문장을 완성하시오.

1 그들은 지난 토요일에 박물관에 있지 않았다. (they, at the museum)
   = _____ last Saturday.

2 Scott은 두 시간 전에 너와 함께 있었니? (Scott, with you)
   = _____ two hours ago?

3 그 상자는 비어 있었다. (the box, empty)
   = _____ .

4 저 여자들은 농구선수였니? (those women, basketball players)
   = _____ ?

A   괄호 안에서 알맞은 것을 고르시오.

1   There (is / are) a smartphone on the bed.

2   (Is / Are) there six birds in the sky?

3   There (wasn't / weren't) many visitors last year.

4   There (was / were) much honey in the jar.

B   다음 문장을 괄호 안의 지시대로 바꿔 쓰시오. (단, 부정문에서는 줄임말을 쓰시오.)

1   There is enough money for us. (부정문으로)   → _____ for us.

2   There are five floors in this building. (의문문으로)   → _____ in this building?

3   There were many trees near my house. (부정문으로)   → _____ near my house.

4   There was a bus stop on this street. (의문문으로)   → _____ on this street?

C   우리말과 같도록 괄호 안의 말을 알맞게 배열하시오.

1   오늘 축구 경기가 있다. (a soccer match, is, there)

   = _____ today.

2   너의 반에 학생 20명이 있니? (are, there, 20 students)

   = _____ in your class?

3   거실에 에어컨 두 대가 있었다. (there, two air conditioners, were)

   = _____ in the living room.

D   우리말과 같도록 there와 괄호 안의 말을 활용하여 문장을 완성하시오.

1   지붕 위에 깃발이 있었니? (a flag)

   = _____ on the roof?

2   그녀의 가방 안에 공책이 전혀 없다. (any notebooks)

   = _____ in her bag.

3   식탁 위에 숟가락 다섯 개가 있니? (five spoons)

   = _____ on the table?

4   테마파크에 많은 아이들이 있었다. (many children)

   = _____ at the theme park.

Writing Exercise +

Answers p.16

A 다음 빈칸에 알맞은 말을 <보기>에서 한 번씩만 골라 쓰시오.

<보기>	is	are	was	were

1 _____ you at church now?

2 Crystal _____ short five years ago.

3 They _____ with Ms. Moore yesterday.

4 _____ the weather cool today?

<보기>	isn't	aren't	wasn't	weren't

5 The babies _____ sleepy now.

6 Thomas _____ sick last Monday.

7 My aunt _____ a news reporter.

8 There _____ any flowers here a year ago.

B 괄호 안의 말과 be동사를 활용하여 대화를 완성하시오.

1 *A*: _____ ready for the test? (you and Silvia)
   B: No, _____.

2 *A*: _____ on vacation last week? (Henry and Jerry)
   B: Yes, _____.

3 *A*: _____ an elementary school student now? (your brother)
   B: Yes, _____.

4 *A*: _____ in the office an hour ago? (Ms. Davis)
   B: No, _____.

5 *A*: _____ in the basket yesterday? (the apples)
   B: No, _____.

C 우리말과 같도록 괄호 안의 말과 be동사를 활용하여 문장을 완성하시오.

1 너는 지금 목마르니? (you, thirsty)

= _____ now?

2 그 수학 시험은 쉽지 않았다. (the math test, easy)

= _____ .

3 이 건물 안에 체육관이 있다. (there, a gym)

= _____ in this building.

4 우리는 어제 피곤하지 않았다. (we, tired)

= _____ yesterday.

5 그는 열두 살이니? (he, twelve years old)

= _____ ?

6 Lisa는 세 시간 전에 수영장에 있었다. (Lisa, in the swimming pool)

= _____ three hours ago.

D 우리말과 같도록 괄호 안의 말을 알맞게 배열하시오.

1 나의 답은 틀리지 않았다. (wrong, not, was, my answer)

= _____ .

2 이 재킷은 일주일 전에 할인 중이었다. (was, this jacket, on sale)

= _____ a week ago.

3 너의 손은 깨끗하니? (clean, your hands, are)

= _____ ?

4 Paul에 집은 산 위에 있다. (is, Paul's house, on the mountain)

= _____ .

5 파티에 사람들이 많지 않았다. (were, many people, there, not)

= _____ at the party.

6 여기에 오래된 서점이 있었니? (an old bookstore, there, was)

= _____ here?

UNIT 01 일반동사의 현재형

Answers p.17

A 괄호 안에서 알맞은 것을 고르시오.

1 Mr. Parker (miss / misses) his old teacher.

2 The baby (crys / cries) loudly at night.

3 My classmate (has / haves) a big backpack.

4 She (gos / goes) to school with her little brother.

5 Alice and I (buy / buys) snacks at this supermarket.

B 괄호 안의 동사를 현재형으로 바꿔 빈칸에 쓰시오.

1 A rabbit _____ very high. (jump)

2 My mom _____ her teeth before bed. (brush)

3 We _____ up at 7:30 in the morning. (get)

4 Mark _____ his laptop on weekdays. (carry)

C 다음 문장을 주어진 주어로 시작하는 문장으로 바꿔 쓰시오.

1 She studies hard for the test.
→ Josh and I _____.

2 We listen to the radio in the evening.
→ Sarah _____.

3 Mr. Baker cleans the room on weekends.
→ The children _____.

D 우리말과 같도록 괄호 안의 말을 활용하여 문장을 완성하시오.

1 이 식물은 많은 물을 필요로 한다. (this plant, need)
= _____ a lot of water.

2 그의 여동생은 방과 후에 요가를 한다. (his sister, do)
= _____ yoga after school.

3 Cindy는 식사 전에 손을 씻는다. (Cindy, wash)
= _____ her hands before meals.

4 저 학생들은 매일 교복을 입는다. (those students, wear)
= _____ school uniforms every day.

UNIT 02　일반동사 현재형의 부정문과 의문문

Answers p.17

A　괄호 안에서 알맞은 것을 고르시오.

1　(Do / Does) they spend time wisely?

2　Mr. Jackson doesn't (live / lives) in Texas.

3　My sister and I (don't / doesn't) share a room.

4　(Do / Does) your uncle have a job?

5　The library (don't / doesn't) close on Saturday.

B　괄호 안의 동사를 활용하여 부정문을 완성하시오. (단, 현재형으로 쓰시오.)

1　She _____ to her family. (lie)

2　Jane and Sam _____ with me. (agree)

3　We _____ the magic shows. (enjoy)

4　That building _____ an elevator. (have)

C　괄호 안의 동사를 활용하여 대화를 완성하시오. (단, 현재형으로 쓰시오.)

1　A: _____ he _____ slowly? (talk)

　　B: No, he _____.

2　A: _____ you _____ that song? (like)

　　B: Yes, I _____.

3　A: _____ Jennifer _____ for her parents after school? (wait)

　　B: Yes, she _____.

D　우리말과 같도록 괄호 안의 말을 활용하여 문장을 완성하시오.

1　너는 그들의 이야기를 믿니? (you, believe)

　　= _____ their story?

2　Henry는 사촌이 있니? (Henry, have)

　　= _____ cousins?

3　그의 아버지는 패스트푸드를 드시지 않는다. (his father, eat)

　　= _____ fast food.

4　나는 학교에서 스마트폰을 사용하지 않는다. (I, use)

　　= _____ smartphones at school.

UNIT 03 일반동사의 과거형

Answers p.17

A 괄호 안에서 알맞은 것을 고르시오.

1 He (doed / did) the laundry 20 minutes ago.

2 I (enjoyed / enjoy) the play last week.

3 She (woke / waked) up at 8 o'clock.

4 Tyler (drops / dropped) the mirror on the floor yesterday.

5 They (worryed / worried) about the dance contest.

B 괄호 안의 동사를 과거형으로 바꿔 빈칸에 쓰시오.

1 The doctor _____ my life two years ago. (save)

2 She _____ Mr. Davis last month. (marry)

3 Lisa _____ Christmas cards yesterday. (write)

4 He _____ a sandwich for breakfast. (have)

C 다음 문장에서 틀린 부분을 바르게 고쳐 완전한 문장을 쓰시오.

1 My sister helps me last week.

→ _____ .

2 We planed the party last Sunday.

→ _____ .

3 He tells a secret to us yesterday.

→ _____ .

4 She drinked much coffee three hours ago.

→ _____ .

D 우리말과 같도록 괄호 안의 말을 활용하여 문장을 완성하시오.

1 John은 어젯밤에 나에게 전화했다. (John, call)

= _____ me last night.

2 Betty는 한 시간 전에 많이 울었다. (Betty, cry)

= _____ a lot an hour ago.

3 그 여자는 어제 꽃을 샀다. (the woman, buy)

= _____ flowers yesterday.

4 그들은 10분 전에 그들의 자리에 앉았다. (they, sit)

= _____ on their seats ten minutes ago.

A 괄호 안에서 알맞은 것을 고르시오.

1 Did Amy (arrive / arrives) on time?

2 (Does / Did) he fix his camera last week?

3 Mr. Martin didn't (buy / bought) a new jacket.

4 The kids (don't / didn't) play together yesterday.

B 괄호 안의 동사를 활용하여 부정문을 완성하시오. (단, 과거형으로 쓰시오.)

1 He _____ at the mall. (shop)

2 Susan _____ the plants last week. (water)

3 I _____ the question. (understand)

4 Matt and Daniel _____ their homework yesterday. (finish)

C 괄호 안의 말을 활용하여 대화를 완성하시오.

1 A: _____ a message to you yesterday? (Sam, send)
  B: No, he _____.

2 A: _____ the science club a year ago? (the boys, join)
  B: No, they _____.

3 A: _____ to the beach last summer? (you, go)
  B: Yes, I _____.

D 우리말과 같도록 괄호 안의 말을 활용하여 문장을 완성하시오.

1 Judy는 도서관에서 책을 빌렸니? (Judy, borrow)
  = _____ books from the library?

2 그 빵집은 어제 일찍 문을 닫았니? (the bakery, close)
  = _____ early yesterday?

3 그의 아들은 오늘 아침에 신문을 읽지 않았다. (his son, read)
  = _____ the newspaper this morning.

4 Olivia와 나는 시험에서 좋은 성적을 받지 못했다. (Olivia and I, get)
  = _____ good grades on the test.

Writing Exercise +

A 다음 문장의 밑줄 친 부분을 바르게 고쳐 쓰시오.

1 Reina <u>finded</u> my pen yesterday. → _____

2 Jerry <u>swimmed</u> in the pool an hour ago. → _____

3 He <u>don't</u> have a pet. → _____

4 Does she <u>needs</u> more time? → _____

5 <u>Do</u> you plant these flowers two weeks ago? → _____

6 Carol <u>uploads</u> videos on YouTube yesterday. → _____

7 Joe <u>carrys</u> his wallet every day. → _____

B 다음 문장을 괄호 안의 지시대로 바꿔 쓰시오. (단, 부정문에서는 줄임말을 쓰시오.)

1 It snowed a lot last winter. (부정문으로)

→ _____ .

2 They change clothes after school. (의문문으로)

→ _____ ?

3 We watch a baseball game on Mondays. (부정문으로)

→ _____ .

4 Simon came from Singapore. (의문문으로)

→ _____ ?

5 My sister met her best friend last Saturday. (부정문으로)

→ _____ .

6 He calls his grandparents every morning. (의문문으로)

→ _____ ?

C 우리말과 같도록 괄호 안의 말을 알맞게 배열하시오.

1 Chris는 나에게 그 이야기를 말해줬다. (the story, Chris, told)

= _____ to me.

2 우리는 그 그림을 만지지 않았다. (did, touch, we, not, the painting)

= _____ .

3 너는 학교에서 역사를 배우니? (learn, you, do, history)

= _____ at school?

4 그는 일기를 쓰지 않는다. (his diary, does, write in, not, he)

= _____ .

5 Rachel은 어제 비행기를 놓쳤니? (miss, Rachel, the flight, did)

= _____ yesterday?

6 나의 아빠는 주말에 그의 차를 세차하신다. (his car, washes, my dad)

= _____ on the weekend.

D 우리말과 같도록 괄호 안의 말을 활용하여 문장을 완성하시오.

1 그는 매운 음식을 좋아하니? (like, spicy food)

= _____ ?

2 우리는 거실에서 그녀의 목소리를 들었다. (hear, her voice)

= _____ in the living room.

3 너는 병원에서 Wood씨를 봤니? (see, Mr. Wood)

= _____ at the hospital?

4 Mary는 매일 저녁 식사를 요리하니? (cook, dinner)

= _____ every day?

5 나의 친구들은 나쁜 말을 하지 않는다. (say, bad words)

= _____ .

6 그녀는 어제 나에게 그 열쇠를 주지 않았다. (give, the key)

= _____ to me yesterday.

UNIT 01 형용사

Answers p.18

A 괄호 안에서 알맞은 것을 고르시오.

1 The clown has a (red nose / nose red).

2 My parents are (health / healthy).

3 She didn't bring (some / any) clothes.

B 괄호 안의 형용사를 알맞은 곳에 넣어 완전한 문장을 쓰시오.

1 They got information. (some) → _____.

2 Laura wanted something. (different) → _____.

3 There is a garden. (beautiful) → _____.

C 우리말과 같도록 <보기>의 형용사와 괄호 안의 명사를 활용하여 문장을 완성하시오.

<보기>	many	much	some	any

1 Scott과 나는 생선을 전혀 먹지 않는다. (fish)

= Scott and I don't eat _____.

2 우리는 숲에서 몇 마리의 새들을 봤다. (birds)

= We saw _____ in the forest.

3 한국에는 많은 도시들이 있다. (cities)

= There are _____ in Korea.

4 그 제빵사는 많은 설탕을 사용하지 않는다. (sugar)

= The baker doesn't use _____.

D 우리말과 같도록 괄호 안의 말을 알맞게 배열하시오.

1 나는 잘못된 무언가를 하지 않았다. (wrong, anything)

= I didn't do _____.

2 그는 짧은 이야기를 썼다. (short, story)

= He wrote a _____.

3 Emma는 흥미로운 무언가를 찾았다. (interesting, something)

= Emma found _____.

UNIT 02 부사

A 밑줄 친 부사가 수식하는 것을 <보기>에서 골라 그 기호를 쓰시오.

| <보기> | ⓐ 동사 | ⓑ 형용사 | ⓒ 다른 부사 | ⓓ 문장 전체 |

1 That restaurant is <u>so</u> famous.   [   ]

2 The man walked <u>very</u> quickly.   [   ]

3 <u>Amazingly</u>, this tree is a hundred years old.   [   ]

4 Jonathan sang <u>beautifully</u> yesterday.   [   ]

B 괄호 안에서 알맞은 것을 고르시오.

1 The helicopter flies (high / highly).

2 They lived (happy / happily) in the country.

3 (Lucky / Luckily), I arrived at the station on time.

4 Her food (is always / always is) too sweet.

5 Tony got up (late / lately) this morning.

C 괄호 안의 빈도부사를 알맞은 곳에 넣어 완전한 문장을 쓰시오.

1 Eddie is shy. (sometimes)   → _____.

2 It rains a lot in Korea. (often)   → _____.

3 They are quiet in class. (never)   → _____.

4 I clean my room on the weekend. (usually)   → _____.

D 우리말과 같도록 괄호 안의 말을 활용하여 빈칸에 쓰시오.

1 나는 안전하게 돌아왔다. (safe)

= I came back _____.

2 그는 조용히 그 비밀을 말했다. (quiet)

= He told the secret _____.

3 그들은 그 시험을 위해 열심히 공부했다. (hard)

= They studied _____ for the exam.

4 Camila와 나는 항상 신문을 읽는다. (always, read)

= Camila and I _____ _____ the newspaper.

A 밑줄 친 부분이 어법상 맞으면 O를 쓰고, 틀리면 바르게 고쳐 쓰시오.

1 Annie doesn't want <u>some</u> advice. → _____

2 He has a <u>love</u> brother. → _____

3 The cook needs <u>many</u> vegetables. → _____

4 The boy throws the ball <u>highly</u>. → _____

5 We didn't sleep <u>good</u> last night. → _____

6 Mr. Jackson <u>often drives</u> his car to work. → _____

7 I didn't hear <u>strange anything</u> yesterday. → _____

8 Her sister solved the problem <u>wise</u>. → _____

B 괄호 안의 말을 빈칸에 알맞은 형태로 쓰시오.

1 (slow)   ① Turtles move _____ .
        ② My computer is very _____ .

2 (gentle)   ① Mike is a _____ boy.
         ② He smiled at me _____ .

3 (careful)   ① She listened _____ to the teacher.
          ② I'm _____ in the kitchen.

4 (surprising)   ① She read the _____ article.
            ② _____ , he won the championship.

5 (fast)   ① The taxi ran _____ .
        ② The song has a _____ rhythm.

6 (early)   ① The sun rises _____ in summer.
         ② I did yoga in the _____ morning.

C 우리말과 같도록 괄호 안의 말을 활용하여 문장을 완성하시오.

1 이 스웨터는 따뜻해 보인다. (warm)

= This sweater looks _____.

2 그 프라이드 치킨은 아주 맛있었다. (real)

= The fried chicken was _____ tasty.

3 Mia는 거의 엘리베이터를 타지 않는다. (takes)

= Mia _____ an elevator.

4 Larry는 공원에서 많은 사슴들을 봤다. (deer)

= Larry saw _____ in the park.

5 그 축구 경기는 늦게 시작했다. (late)

= The soccer match started _____.

6 나는 악기를 전혀 연주하지 않는다. (musical instruments)

= I don't play _____.

D 우리말과 같도록 괄호 안의 말을 알맞게 배열하시오.

1 그 영화는 매우 놀라웠다. (amazing, very, was)

= The movie _____.

2 그는 많은 돈을 가지고 있지 않다. (doesn't, money, much, have)

= He _____.

3 그 카페는 인기 있는 디저트를 판다. (desserts, popular, sells)

= The café _____.

4 Angela는 보통 학교에서 안경을 쓴다. (wears, usually, glasses)

= Angela _____ at school.

5 Moore씨는 나에게 약간의 오렌지 주스를 주셨다. (gave, orange juice, some)

= Mr. Moore _____ to me.

6 우리는 지난 월요일에 재미있는 무언가를 계획했다. (fun, something, planned)

= We _____ last Monday.

UNIT 01   현재진행시제

Answers p.18

A   괄호 안에서 알맞은 것을 고르시오.

1 Thomas is (brush / brushing) his teeth.

2 I (am not talking / am talking not) about you.

3 They are (puting / putting) posters on the wall.

4 Is (using Sally / Sally using) the phone?

5 Are you (tying / tieing) a ribbon around the box?

B   다음 문장을 괄호 안의 지시대로 바꿔 쓰시오.

1 They are eating ice cream. (의문문으로)

→ _____ ice cream?

2 Mr. Olson is parking a car. (부정문으로)

→ _____ a car.

3 I am looking at the butterfly. (부정문으로)

→ _____ at the butterfly.

4 My sister is choosing a present for me. (의문문으로)

→ _____ a present for me?

C   <보기>의 동사를 한 번씩만 활용하여 빈칸에 쓰시오. (단, 현재진행시제로 쓰시오.)

<보기>   draw   swim   take

1 _____ the man _____ a shower?

2 _____ you and Carl _____ cartoons?

3 _____ Susan _____ in the pool now?

D   우리말과 같도록 괄호 안의 동사를 활용하여 문장을 완성하시오.

1 Robert는 잔디 위에 누워 있지 않다. (lie)

= _____ on the grass.

2 그녀는 빵을 굽고 있다. (bake)

= _____ bread.

3 너는 그에게 문자 메시지를 보내고 있니? (send)

= _____ a text message to him?

UNIT 02 미래시제

A 괄호 안에서 알맞은 것을 고르시오.

1 The event (won't / not will) begin next month.

2 We (are going not / aren't going) to go to the movies.

3 Judy will (prepare / preparing) for the marathon.

4 (Will / Are) you going to order coffee?

B <보기>의 동사와 괄호 안의 말을 한 번씩만 활용하여 문장을 완성하시오.

<보기>	change	practice	buy

1 She _____ the piano after breakfast. (will)

2 _____ you _____ a new laptop? (be going to)

3 Paul _____ his mind. (not, will)

C 다음 문장을 괄호 안의 말을 활용하여 미래시제로 바꿔 쓰시오.

1 Does she like this doll? (will)

→ _____ this doll?

2 He is busy today. (be going to)

→ _____ tomorrow.

3 Do you eat out every weekend? (be going to)

→ _____ out this weekend?

4 Helen doesn't exercise at the gym. (will)

→ _____ at the gym.

D 우리말과 같도록 괄호 안의 말을 활용하여 문장을 완성하시오.

1 Mandy는 그와 결혼할 거니? (be going to, marry)

= _____ him?

2 Daniel은 나를 용서하지 않을 것이다. (will, forgive)

= _____ me.

3 그들은 다음 학기에 독서 동아리에 가입할 거니? (will, join)

= _____ the book club next semester?

Writing Exercise ✚

A 밑줄 친 부분이 어법상 맞으면 O를 쓰고, 틀리면 바르게 고쳐 쓰시오.

1 My mom is checking not the mailbox. → _____

2 The city tour is going to be exciting. → _____

3 He not will have dessert tonight. → _____

4 Mr. Nelson will proposes to his girlfriend this weekend. → _____

5 Are they go to borrow a camera? → _____

6 Andy is riding the roller coaster now. → _____

7 Will Cynthia bringing some snacks to the picnic? → _____

8 It is going to not snow next Monday. → _____

B 다음 문장을 괄호 안의 지시대로 바꿔 쓰시오.

1 She will be angry at us. (의문문으로)
→ _____ angry at us?

2 I will forget her name later. (부정문으로)
→ _____ her name later.

3 They are planning Tom's birthday party. (의문문으로)
→ _____ Tom's birthday party?

4 Jenny is listening to the radio. (부정문으로)
→ _____ to the radio.

5 He is going to see the dentist next month. (의문문으로)
→ _____ the dentist next month?

6 My friends are going to go to the aquarium. (부정문으로)
→ _____ to the aquarium.

C 우리말과 같도록 괄호 안의 말을 활용하여 문장을 완성하시오.

1 Bob은 지금 도서관에서 공부하고 있니? (study)

= _____ in the library now?

2 너는 저 파일들을 다운로드할 거니? (will, download)

= _____ those files?

3 그들은 슈퍼마켓에서 쇼핑하고 있다. (shop)

= _____ at the supermarket.

4 Amanda는 장난감 가게를 방문하지 않을 것이다. (will, visit)

= _____ the toy store.

5 우리는 곧 초등학교를 졸업할 것이다. (be going to, graduate)

= _____ from elementary school soon.

D 우리말과 같도록 괄호 안의 말을 알맞게 배열하시오.

1 다음 주에 바람이 많이 불 거니? (windy, will, be, it)

= _____ next week?

2 그 아기들은 지금 울고 있지 않다. (crying, are, the babies, not)

= _____ now.

3 Linda는 오늘 머리를 자를 것이다. (Linda, her hair, cut, going to, is)

= _____ today.

4 우리는 우리의 시간을 낭비하지 않을 것이다. (our time, not, will, waste, we)

= _____ .

5 나의 형은 그의 친구와 악수하고 있다. (is, hands, my brother, shaking)

= _____ with his friend.

6 Jeffrey는 내일 너를 도와줄 거니? (going to, Jeffrey, help, is, you)

= _____ tomorrow?

7 나는 같은 실수를 하지 않을 것이다. (am, the same mistake, going to, not, make, I)

= _____ .

UNIT 01 can, may

Answers p.19

A 괄호 안에서 알맞은 것을 고르시오.

1 My brother may (pass / passes) the exam.

2 You (take may / may take) a taxi.

3 She (can't / not can) meet you today.

4 Can (bring I / I bring) my pet there?

B 밑줄 친 부분의 의미를 <보기>에서 골라 그 기호를 쓰시오.

> <보기>   ⓐ ~할 수 있다   ⓑ ~해도 된다   ⓒ ~일지도 모른다

1 May I cut this cake?   [   ]

2 Her parrot can say some words.   [   ]

3 That man may be Mr. Thompson.   [   ]

4 Can I sit next to you?   [   ]

C <보기>의 동사와 괄호 안의 말을 활용하여 문장을 완성하시오.

> <보기>   arrive   know   buy   invite

1 Paul is very smart. He _____ the answer. (may)

2 I don't have enough money. I _____ that necklace. (can)

3 Tomorrow is your birthday. You _____ your friends. (may)

4 We left home early. We _____ at the airport on time. (can)

D 우리말과 같도록 괄호 안의 말을 활용하여 문장을 완성하시오.

1 내가 계획을 바꿔도 되니? (I, change)

= _____ the plan?

2 나의 남동생은 저 상자를 들 수 없다. (my brother, lift)

= _____ that box.

3 Green씨는 은행에 있을지도 모른다. (Ms. Green, be)

= _____ in the bank.

UNIT 02   must, have to

Answers p.19

A 괄호 안에서 알맞은 것을 고르시오.

1 We must (eat / to eat) more vegetables.

2 Carol (don't / doesn't) have to fix the machine.

3 Bob and his brother (has / have) to go to the dentist.

4 You must (throw not / not throw) away the trash on the street.

B 다음 빈칸에 must not과 don't/doesn't have to 중 알맞은 것을 쓰시오.

1 This is a secret. You _____ tell anyone.

2 My uncle will drive me to school. I _____ take the bus.

3 The baby is sleeping now. We _____ make noise.

4 Jason _____ read the book. He already knows the story.

C 괄호 안의 말을 활용하여 문장을 완성하시오.

1 Your desk is always dirty. You _____ it every day. (must, clean)

2 Ms. Miller _____ dinner. Her family will eat out tonight. (have to, cook)

3 Robert _____ Amy. He has a gift for her. (have to, visit)

4 You _____ on the bus. You may spill the food. (must, eat)

D 우리말과 같도록 괄호 안의 말을 알맞게 배열하시오.

1 우리는 밤에 수영하면 안 된다. (not, we, swim, must)

= _____ at night.

2 Janet은 그녀의 옷을 갈아입어야 한다. (change, Janet, to, has)

= _____ her clothes.

3 학생들은 학교에서 그들의 스마트폰을 꺼야 한다. (turn off, must, students)

= _____ their smartphones at school.

4 너는 새 신발을 살 필요가 없다. (have, buy, to, don't, you)

= _____ new shoes.

Writing Exercise ✚

A 밑줄 친 부분이 어법상 맞으면 O를 쓰고, 틀리면 바르게 고쳐 쓰시오.

1 Marco <u>come may</u> from Italy. → _____

2 Sally <u>have to</u> trust her friends. → _____

3 Can Alex <u>teaches</u> us soccer? → _____

4 They <u>must win</u> this game. → _____

5 <u>May I drink</u> some coke? → _____

6 You <u>not must</u> skip breakfast. → _____

7 He <u>cannot ride</u> a horse. → _____

8 She <u>doesn't has to</u> write a book report. → _____

B <보기>의 동사와 괄호 안의 말을 활용하여 대화를 완성하시오.

<보기>	leave	go	wear	be	understand

1 A: Ashley has bad eyesight.
   B: Yes. She _____ glasses. (have to)

2 A: _____ you _____ Korean? (can)
   B: No. I only speak Chinese.

3 A: You _____ food on your plate. (must)
   B: But I'm really full.

4 A: I'm sorry. I _____ to the party. (can)
   B: Why? Are you busy on that day?

5 A: Did you see Andy today?
   B: He _____ in the art room. The drawing contest is tomorrow. (may)

C 우리말과 같도록 괄호 안의 동사를 활용하여 빈칸에 쓰시오.

1 Parker씨는 이 약을 먹어야 한다. (take)

= Mr. Parker _____ _____ this medicine.

2 너는 한 시간 동안 TV를 봐도 된다. (watch)

= You _____ _____ TV for an hour.

3 그는 아이스하키를 할 수 있니? (play)

= _____ he _____ ice hockey?

4 우리는 계단을 오를 필요가 없다. (climb)

= We _____ _____ _____ _____ the stairs.

5 Beth는 오늘 그녀의 숙제를 끝낼 수 없다. (finish)

= Beth _____ _____ her homework today.

6 학생들은 이 수업에서 영어를 사용해야 한다. (use)

= Students _____ _____ _____ English in this class.

D 우리말과 같도록 괄호 안의 말을 알맞게 배열하시오.

1 내가 정원에 꽃을 심어도 되니? (I, flowers, plant, can)

= _____ in the garden?

2 그들은 이 건물에 들어오면 안 된다. (enter, not, they, this building, must)

= _____.

3 그녀는 나의 이름을 알지도 모른다. (she, my name, know, may)

= _____.

4 내가 과학 동아리에 가입해도 되니? (join, I, the science club, may)

= _____?

5 너는 나의 노트북을 빌려도 된다. (borrow, you, my laptop, can)

= _____.

6 Tom은 나에게 이메일을 보낼 필요가 없다. (send, have, an e-mail, doesn't, Tom, to)

= _____ to me.

UNIT 01   감각동사

Answers p.20

A   괄호 안에서 알맞은 것을 고르시오.

1 These towels smell (nice / nicely).

2 This pillow (feels / tastes) like silk.

3 My grandfather looks (health / healthy).

4 That (sounds / sounds like) a siren.

5 The doughnut tastes (amazing / amazingly).

B   <보기>의 동사를 한 번씩만 활용하여 문장을 완성하시오. (단, 과거형으로 쓰시오.)

<보기>   look   sound   taste   feel

1 His story _____ boring.

2 The shadow _____ a ghost.

3 Macy _____ nervous at the audition.

4 That chocolate _____ bitter.

C   괄호 안의 말을 알맞게 배열하시오.

1 _____. (looks, this puzzle, difficult)

2 _____. (the perfume, good, smells)

3 _____. (like, the cookie, blueberries, tastes)

4 _____. (sounded, her answer, perfect)

D   우리말과 같도록 괄호 안의 말을 활용하여 문장을 완성하시오.

1 그의 음식은 항상 짠맛이 난다. (salty)

  = His food always _____.

2 나는 마라톤 후에 목마르게 느꼈다. (thirsty)

  = I _____ after the marathon.

3 이 비누는 장미 같은 냄새가 난다. (roses)

  = This soap _____.

4 그 롤러코스터는 안전해 보인다. (safe)

  = The roller coaster _____.

UNIT 02 수여동사

A 괄호 안에서 알맞은 것을 고르시오.

1 Mr. Collins taught (art us / us art).

2 They will build a gym (to / for) the students.

3 He bought (us / for us) dinner yesterday.

B 다음 빈칸에 알맞은 동사를 <보기>에서 한 번씩만 골라 쓰시오. (단, 과거형으로 쓰시오.)

<보기>	tell	pass	send	make

1 I _____ a postcard to Rachel.

2 She _____ cupcakes for the children.

3 The waiter _____ him a cup of coffee.

4 Edward _____ his friend the answer.

C <보기>와 같이 다음 두 문장의 의미가 같도록 문장을 완성하시오.

<보기>	Romeo gave her a box. → Romeo *gave a box to her* .

1 She lent her brother some money.   → She _____ .

2 Jake got a chair for the new student.   → Jake _____ .

3 The librarian will find me the book.   → The librarian _____ .

D 우리말과 같도록 괄호 안의 말을 알맞게 배열하시오.

1 엄마는 우리에게 피자를 요리해주셨다. (cooked, pizza, us)

= Mom _____ .

2 그녀는 그녀의 아버지께 몇몇 질문을 했다. (some questions, her father, asked, of)

= She _____ .

3 Tony는 나에게 시계를 줬다. (me, gave, a watch)

= Tony _____ .

4 Tina는 아픈 사람들에게 신문을 읽어줄 것이다. (will read, sick people, to, newspapers)

= Tina _____ .

Writing Exercise ✛

Answers p.20

A 밑줄 친 부분이 어법상 맞으면 O를 쓰고, 틀리면 바르게 고쳐 쓰시오.

1 I bought a necklace <u>to</u> her. → _____

2 His music sounded <u>love</u>. → _____

3 It <u>smells</u> an old house. → _____

4 Ms. Green told <u>us funny jokes</u>. → _____

5 Janet feels <u>happily</u> today. → _____

6 Jim lent <u>a bicycle me</u>. → _____

7 She <u>looks like</u> a model. → _____

8 My parents give much love <u>for</u> me. → _____

B <보기>의 동사를 한 번씩만 활용하여 문장을 완성하시오. (단, 과거형으로 쓰시오.)

<보기>	sound	taste	feel

1 The sand _____ soft.

2 The watermelon _____ sweet.

3 His voice _____ my brother's voice.

<보기>	write	cook	get

4 The boy _____ her a letter.

5 She _____ the ticket for me.

6 Ms. Nelson _____ her cat special food.

C 우리말과 같도록 괄호 안의 말을 활용하여 빈칸에 쓰시오.

1 이 우유는 상한 냄새가 난다. (smell, bad)

= This milk _____ _____ .

2 아보카도는 버터 같은 맛이 난다. (taste, butter)

= Avocados _____ _____ _____ .

3 그녀는 그들에게 샌드위치를 만들어줬다. (make, sandwiches)

= She _____ _____ _____ .

4 Amy는 때때로 외롭게 느낀다. (feel, lonely)

= Amy sometimes _____ _____ .

5 엄마는 나에게 오래된 사진들을 보내주셨다. (send, old pictures)

= Mom _____ _____ _____ _____ .

6 그는 그의 친구에게 새 스마트폰을 보여줬다. (show, a new smartphone)

= He _____ _____ _____ _____ _____ .

D 우리말과 같도록 괄호 안의 말을 알맞게 배열하시오.

1 너의 고모는 젊어 보이신다. (young, looks, your aunt)

= _____ .

2 Jerry는 Megan에게 숟가락을 건네줬다. (passed, Jerry, the spoon, Megan)

= _____ .

3 그들은 방문객들에게 작은 선물을 가져다줬다. (the visitors, small gifts, they, to, brought)

= _____ .

4 그 뉴스는 거짓말처럼 들렸다. (a lie, like, sounded, the news)

= _____ .

5 Lee씨는 외국인들에게 한국어를 가르쳐준다. (foreigners, teaches, to, Korean, Ms. Lee)

= _____ .

6 기자들은 그 가수에게 많은 질문을 했다. (the singer, the reporters, many questions, asked)

= _____ .

UNIT 01 장소를 나타내는 전치사

Answers p.20

A 괄호 안에서 알맞은 것을 고르시오.

1 Edward will arrive (at / on) the airport soon.

2 Your shoes are (in / under) the desk.

3 The girl dropped the earphones (in / on) the floor.

4 There was a big dog behind (they / them).

B 다음 빈칸에 알맞은 전치사를 <보기>에서 한 번씩만 골라 쓰시오.

<보기>	at	in	on	next to

1 I am wearing a ring _____ my finger.

2 My brother and I usually study _____ home.

3 There is a supermarket _____ the bakery.

4 Sophia bought this chocolate _____ Switzerland.

C 우리말과 같도록 괄호 안의 말을 활용하여 문장을 완성하시오.

1 그 차는 내 앞에 섰다. (me)
 = The car stopped _____.

2 그는 가방 안에 그의 교과서를 넣었다. (the bag)
 = He put his textbooks _____.

3 그 관광객들은 가이드 뒤에서 걷고 있다. (the guide)
 = The tourists are walking _____.

D 우리말과 같도록 괄호 안의 말을 알맞게 배열하시오.

1 그들은 버스 정류장에서 Tina를 기다릴 것이다. (the bus stop, Tina, at)
 = They are going to wait for _____.

2 나는 그의 옆에서 음악을 들었다. (him, next, music, to)
 = I listened to _____.

3 Sharon은 그녀의 바지에 물을 쏟았다. (on, water, her pants)
 = Sharon spilled _____.

UNIT 02 시간을 나타내는 전치사

A 괄호 안에서 알맞은 것을 고르시오.

1 Flowers are beautiful (in / on) April.

2 Summer comes (after / before) spring.

3 The musical finished (in / at) 8:30.

4 You can play computer games (for / during) three hours.

B 다음 빈칸에 for와 during 중 알맞은 것을 쓰시오.

1 Frank and I laughed _____ the TV show.

2 They were in the hospital _____ 20 days.

3 She will practice taekwondo _____ an hour.

4 I'm going to visit my grandparents _____ the holidays.

C 다음 대화의 빈칸에 알맞은 전치사를 <보기>에서 한 번씩만 골라 쓰시오.

<보기>	on	in	before	during

1 A: Do you go to sleep early?   B: Yes. I usually go to sleep _____ 9 P.M.

2 A: Do you live in Suwon?   B: No. I moved to Yongin _____ 2012.

3 A: Did you take pictures _____ the picnic?   B: No. I didn't bring my camera.

4 A: Do you have any hobbies?   B: Yes. I play tennis _____ Fridays.

D 우리말과 같도록 괄호 안의 말을 활용하여 문장을 완성하시오.

1 Emma는 그녀의 생일에 우리를 초대했다. (her birthday)
  = Emma invited us _____.

2 그 기차는 4시 전에 떠날 것이다. (4 o'clock)
  = The train will leave _____.

3 그들은 저녁 식사 후에 영화를 보러 갔다. (dinner)
  = They went to the movies _____.

4 Parker씨는 세 달 동안 사막을 여행했다. (three months)
  = Mr. Parker traveled the desert _____.

Writing Exercise +

Answers p.21

A 밑줄 친 부분이 어법상 맞으면 O를 쓰고, 틀리면 at, in, on 중 하나로 고쳐 쓰시오.

1 John rested <u>in</u> home yesterday. → _____

2 My father is working <u>at</u> Germany now. → _____

3 They will eat cake <u>in</u> Christmas Eve. → _____

4 Mom watches TV drama <u>in</u> the evening. → _____

5 She sent me the text message <u>on</u> night. → _____

6 My jacket is <u>on</u> the chair. → _____

B 다음 대화의 빈칸에 알맞은 전치사를 <보기>에서 한 번씩만 골라 쓰시오.

<보기>	at	in	under	before	for

1 *A*: Are you enjoying your vacation?
   B: Yes. I'm spending time with my family _____ Sokcho.

2 *A*: Did you find my puppies?
   B: Yes. They were _____ the bed.

3 *A*: Does he know about England well?
   B: Yes. He lived in England _____ eight years.

4 *A*: Will you return the books?
   B: Yes. I will return them _____ the weekend.

5 *A*: Does the train stop here?
   B: No. It stops _____ the next station.

C 우리말과 같도록 괄호 안의 말을 활용하여 문장을 완성하시오.

1 우리는 어제 두 시간 동안 수다를 떨었다. (two hours)

= We chatted _____ yesterday.

2 그녀는 종이 위에 그림을 그리고 있다. (the paper)

= She is drawing a picture _____.

3 너는 점심 식사 전에 나에게 전화해도 된다. (lunch)

= You can call me _____.

4 그 강은 다리 아래에서 흐른다. (the bridge)

= The river flows _____.

5 Adam은 매일 방과 후에 운동한다. (school)

= Adam exercises _____ every day.

6 그 학생들은 미술관 앞에서 그들의 선생님을 만났다. (the art museum)

= The students met their teacher _____.

D 우리말과 같도록 괄호 안의 말을 알맞게 배열하시오.

1 포르투갈은 스페인 옆에 있다. (to, is, Spain, next)

= Portugal _____.

2 한국 사람들은 추석에 송편을 먹는다. (Chuseok, eat, on, songpyeon)

= Koreans _____.

3 Brown씨는 그 건물 뒤에 주차했다. (the building, behind, parked)

= Mr. Brown _____.

4 그녀는 여행 동안 자석들을 모았다. (magnets, the trip, collected, during)

= She _____.

5 그 아이들은 벤치에 앉아 있다. (are sitting, the bench, on)

= The children _____.

6 벨은 1876년에 전화기를 발명했다. (1876, the telephone, invented, in)

= Bell _____.

UNIT 01 and, but, or

Answers p.21

A 괄호 안에서 가장 알맞은 것을 고르시오.

1 She woke up early (and / or) took the first bus.

2 Is the teacher in the classroom (and / or) in the office?

3 There are notebooks, textbooks, (but / and) some coins in my bag.

4 Josh ordered coke, (or / but) the staff gave him sparkling water.

B 다음 빈칸에 가장 알맞은 말을 괄호 안에서 한 번씩만 골라 쓰시오.

1 (and / or) ① The baby can read _____ write.

② Will you play outside _____ stay at home?

2 (but / or) ① Do you have a pen _____ a pencil?

② Charlie's family was poor _____ happy.

3 (and / but) ① I know that girl, _____ she doesn't know me.

② She usually eats bread _____ butter for breakfast.

C <보기>에서 가장 알맞은 접속사를 한 번씩만 골라 다음 두 문장을 한 문장으로 연결하시오.

<보기>	and	but	or

1 This printer is new. It doesn't work well.

→ This printer is new _____ doesn't work well.

2 It was windy this morning. It was cloudy this morning.

→ It was windy _____ cloudy this morning.

3 You may change your seat today. You may change your seat tomorrow.

→ You may change your seat today _____ tomorrow.

D 우리말과 같도록 괄호 안의 말을 활용하여 빈칸에 쓰시오.

1 그들은 3월이나 4월에 한국으로 여행갈 것이다. (in March, in April)

= They will travel to Korea _____ _____ _____ _____ _____.

2 나의 남동생은 키가 작지만 운동을 잘한다. (short, good at sports)

= My brother is _____ _____ _____ _____ _____.

3 Moore씨는 매일 저녁 식사를 준비하고 설거지를 한다. (prepare dinner, wash the dishes)

= Mr. Moore _____ _____ _____ _____ _____ every day.

UNIT 02 when, before, after, because

Answers p.21

A 괄호 안에서 가장 알맞은 것을 고르시오.

1 You have to write a memo (before / after) you forget it.

2 She got lost (before / because) she didn't have a map.

3 After he (will save / saves) some money, he will buy a new bicycle.

4 Jacob was my classmate (when / because) I was ten years old.

B 괄호 안의 접속사를 이용하여 다음 두 문장을 한 문장으로 연결하시오.

1 Your face turned red. You made a mistake. (after)

→ Your face turned red _____.

2 Jeremy was in the hospital. He had an accident. (because)

→ Jeremy was in the hospital _____.

3 We must look around. We cross the street. (before)

→ We must look around _____.

C 우리말과 같도록 괄호 안의 말을 알맞게 배열하시오.

1 Patrick은 그의 팀이 야구 경기를 진 후에 울었다. (after, lost, his team)

= Patrick cried _____ the baseball game.

2 우리는 운동할 때 많은 물을 마신다. (exercise, we, when)

= We drink a lot of water _____.

3 나는 나의 강아지가 다리를 다쳤기 때문에 슬펐다. (my puppy, because, hurt)

= I was sad _____ its leg.

4 Susan은 어두워지기 전에 역에 도착할 것이다. (gets, it, before)

= Susan will arrive at the station _____ dark.

D 우리말과 같도록 괄호 안의 말을 활용하여 문장을 완성하시오.

1 나는 지금 바쁘기 때문에 너와 이야기할 수 없다. (be, busy)

= I can't talk with you _____ now.

2 그녀는 태양이 밝게 빛날 때 선글라스를 쓴다. (the sun, shine)

= She wears sunglasses _____ brightly.

3 그는 토마토를 씻은 후에 그것들을 자를 것이다. (wash, the tomatoes)

= _____, he will cut them.

Writing Exercise +

Answers p.21

A 다음 빈칸에 가장 알맞은 말을 <보기>에서 한 번씩만 골라 쓰시오.

<보기>	and a coat	but he didn't read them
	or take the subway	when you need my help
	after it became popular	because I can go skiing

1 I like winter _____.

2 He will buy a hat _____.

3 _____, you can call me.

4 He may walk to school _____.

5 Andrew borrowed many books, _____.

6 They watched that movie _____.

B 다음 빈칸에 가장 알맞은 접속사를 <보기>에서 한 번씩만 골라 쓰시오.

<보기>	but	or	when

1 My dog wags its tail _____ it sees me.

2 The pasta was cold _____ tasted good.

3 Can I color this circle red _____ green?

<보기>	and	before	because

4 I was so hungry _____ I skipped breakfast.

5 He had a fever _____ a headache yesterday.

6 Sally stayed in Greece _____ she went to Turkey.

C 우리말과 같도록 괄호 안의 말을 알맞게 배열하시오.

1 그는 그 가게가 문을 열기 전에 줄을 서서 기다렸다. (the store, before, opened)
= He waited in line _____.

2 나는 나의 성적표를 숨겼지만, 나의 어머니는 그것을 찾으셨다. (it, my mother, but, found)
= I hid my report card, _____.

3 Miranda는 그의 노래를 들은 후에 그의 팬이 되었다. (after, his song, listened to, Miranda)
= _____, she became his fan.

4 Samuel은 TV를 보고 컴퓨터 게임을 했다. (computer games, played, and)
= Samuel watched TV _____.

5 아기들이 자고 있기 때문에 너는 조용히 해야 한다. (the babies, because, are sleeping)
= You have to be quiet _____.

6 그의 딸은 어렸을 때 생선을 좋아하지 않았다. (young, she, when, was)
= His daughter didn't like fish _____.

D 우리말과 같도록 괄호 안의 말을 활용하여 문장을 완성하시오.

1 식물들은 물과 햇빛을 필요로 한다. (water, sunlight)
= Plants need _____.

2 그는 늦은 시간까지 깨어있었기 때문에 피곤했다. (stay up late)
= He was tired _____.

3 그들은 비가 그친 후에 소풍을 갈 것이다. (the rain, stop)
= They will go on a picnic _____.

4 너는 바다에서 수영할 때 조심해야 한다. (swim, in the ocean)
= You must be careful _____.

5 우리는 그 수업이 시작하기 전에 잠시 휴식을 취했다. (the class, start)
= We took a break _____.

6 Maria는 나에게 이메일이나 문자 메시지를 보낼 것이다. (an e-mail, a text message)
= Maria will send me _____.

UNIT 01 의문사 의문문 I

Answers p.21

A 괄호 안에서 알맞은 것을 고르시오.

1 (Who / What) is your roommate?

2 (Whom / What) music is Josh listening to?

3 (Whom / Whose) are you meeting?

4 (Who / Whose) notebooks are on the desk?

5 (Who / What) did Alice give you on Valentine's Day?

B 다음 빈칸에 알맞은 의문사를 넣어 주어진 대답의 밑줄 친 부분에 대해 묻는 의문문을 완성하시오.

1 A: _____ baked this cake?   B: My grandmother baked it.

2 A: _____ flowers are they?   B: They are lilies.

3 A: _____ gloves are these?   B: They are Jimmy's gloves.

4 A: _____ is under the sofa?   B: A tennis ball is under the sofa.

C 다음 빈칸에 who와 what 중 알맞은 것을 넣어 대화를 완성하시오.

1 A: _____ wrote this letter to you?   B: My brother wrote it.

2 A: _____ club did they join?   B: They joined the movie club.

3 A: _____ did Gina help yesterday?   B: She helped an old man.

4 A: _____ did Peter do last Sunday?   B: He went to the swimming pool.

D 우리말과 같도록 괄호 안의 말을 알맞게 배열하시오.

1 누가 나의 컴퓨터를 고쳤니? (fixed, who, my computer)

= _____ ?

2 너는 지난주에 무엇을 배웠니? (did, learn, you, what)

= _____ last week?

3 이것은 누구의 전화번호니? (is, phone number, this, whose)

= _____ ?

UNIT 02 의문사 의문문 II

A 괄호 안에서 알맞은 것을 고르시오.

1 *A*: (Where / When) did you put your glasses?
B: I put them in the case.

2 *A*: (How many / How much) is that bicycle?
B: It is $200.

3 *A*: (Why / What time) did she have lunch?
B: She had lunch at 1 P.M.

B 주어진 대답의 밑줄 친 부분에 대해 묻는 의문문을 완성하시오.

1 *A*: _____ did he borrow the books?　　*B*: He borrowed the book two days ago.

2 *A*: _____ does she go to school?　　*B*: She goes to school by bus.

3 *A*: _____ is the post office?　　*B*: It is behind that tall building.

4 *A*: _____ coins are in your purse?　　*B*: There are five coins.

C 다음 대화의 빈칸에 알맞은 말을 <보기>에서 골라 쓰시오.

<보기>　　when　　why　　how far　　how often

1 *A*: _____ is Matt's birthday?　　*B*: It is March 15.

2 *A*: _____ is your house from here?　　*B*: It is four kilometers.

3 *A*: _____ does Ms. Moore drink coffee?　　*B*: Twice a day.

4 *A*: _____ were they late for class?　　*B*: Because the traffic was bad.

D 우리말과 같도록 괄호 안의 말을 알맞게 배열하시오.

1 너는 왜 저녁에 운동하니? (you, do, exercise, why)
= _____ in the evening?

2 거북이는 얼마나 오래 사니? (live, how, turtles, long, do)
= _____?

3 그녀는 어떻게 그 소문을 들었니? (the rumor, did, how, hear, she)
= _____?

A   괄호 안에서 알맞은 것을 고르시오.

1 (Speak / Spoke) in English, please.

2 What a cold day (is it / it is)!

3 (What / How) hard he studies!

4 Let's (don't / not) give up now.

5 (Be / Do) friendly to everyone.

B   다음 빈칸에 알맞은 말을 <보기>에서 한 번씩만 골라 쓰시오.

<보기>	stand up	don't worry	let's eat	let's not play

1 _____ at this restaurant. It looks nice.

2 _____ about the speech contest. I can help you.

3 _____ video games tonight. I'm so tired.

4 _____, please. You have to stretch your body.

C   <보기>와 같이 다음 문장을 괄호 안의 말을 활용하여 감탄문으로 바꿔 쓰시오.

<보기>	It is a very peaceful song. (what)	→ *What a peaceful song* it is!

1 That museum is really big. (how)   → _____ that museum is!

2 Those are really great pictures. (what)   → _____ those are!

3 It rained very heavily. (how)   → _____ it rained!

D   우리말과 같도록 괄호 안의 말을 활용하여 문장을 완성하시오.

1 복도에서 뛰지 마라. (run)

= _____ in the hallway.

2 그들은 정말 영리하구나! (clever)

= _____ they are!

3 눈사람을 만들자. (make)

= _____ a snowman.

4 저것은 정말 놀라운 소식이구나! (surprising news)

= _____ that is!

Writing Exercise +

Answers p.22

A 주어진 대답의 밑줄 친 부분에 대해 묻는 의문문을 완성하시오.

1 A: _____ broke the windows?

B: <u>Jeffrey</u> broke them.

2 A: _____ did you finish your homework?

B: I finished it <u>yesterday</u>.

3 A: _____ is the ticket?

B: It is <u>$12</u>.

4 A: _____ does the bank close today?

B: <u>Because today is a national holiday</u>.

5 A: _____ is your brother?

B: He is <u>17 years old</u>.

6 A: _____ is the bus stop?

B: It is <u>in front of the supermarket</u>.

7 A: _____ name was on the cake?

B: <u>Susan's</u> name was on it.

B 다음 문장을 괄호 안의 지시대로 바꿔 쓰시오.

1 He is a very famous actor. (감탄문으로) → _____!

2 You are shy. (부정 명령문으로) → _____.

3 You bring the sketchbook. (긍정 명령문으로) → _____.

4 She walks very quietly. (감탄문으로) → _____!

5 You touch the screen. (부정 명령문으로) → _____.

6 You lock the door. (긍정 명령문으로) → _____.

7 Those apples are really cheap. (감탄문으로) → _____!

8 You paint on the wall. (부정 명령문으로) → _____.

C 우리말과 같도록 괄호 안의 말을 활용하여 문장을 완성하시오.

1 음악을 꺼라. (turn off)

= _____ the music.

2 너는 왜 태권도를 배우니? (learn)

= _____ taekwondo?

3 과학은 정말 흥미롭구나! (interesting)

= _____ science is!

4 오늘이 며칠이니? (the date)

= _____ today?

5 거짓말하지 말자. (tell)

= _____ a lie.

6 Linda는 공원에서 누구를 봤니? (see)

= _____ at the park?

D 우리말과 같도록 괄호 안의 말을 알맞게 배열하시오.

1 정원에 나무를 심자. (trees, plant, let's)

= _____ in the garden.

2 저 버튼을 누르지 마라. (that button, push, don't)

= _____ .

3 너는 언제 그 노트북을 샀니? (you, when, buy, did, the laptop)

= _____ ?

4 그것은 정말 쉬운 질문이구나! (an, is, question, what, it, easy)

= _____ !

5 그 사고는 어디에서 일어났니? (the accident, where, happen, did)

= _____ ?

6 그 탑은 얼마나 많은 층이 있니? (how, have, the tower, does, floors, many)

= _____ ?

MEMO

MEMO

HACKERS
GRAMMAR
SMART STARTER

WORKBOOK

해커스 그래머 스마트가 특별한 이유!

[Completely master English grammar]

1 누구나 쉽게 이해할 수 있는 **간결한 문법 설명**

2 실생활에서 그대로 사용할 수 있는 **유용한 표현과 예문**

3 '개념 확인' → '연습 문제' → '작문 연습' → '단원 마무리'로 이어지는 **4단계 문제풀이**

[Effectively prepare for middle school English exams]

1 학교 시험 기출경향을 완벽 반영한 문제로 **서술형 포함 내신 완벽 대비**

2 풍부한 문제의 Workbook과 **다양한 부가 학습 자료**로 학습효과 Up Up!

| 해커스 중고등 교재 MAP | 나에게 맞는 교재 선택!

	초5	초6	예비중	중1	중2
문법			Hackers Grammar Smart Starter	Hackers Grammar Smart Level 1	Hackers Grammar Smart Level 2
				기출로 적중 해커스 중학영문법 1학년	기출로 적중 해커스 중학영문법 2학년
				해커스 중학영문법 중간·기말 대비 문제집 Level 1	해커스 중학영문법 중간·기말 대비 문제집 Level 2
서술형				해커스 쓰기 자신감 Level 1	해커스 쓰기 자신감 Level 2
구문					
독해	Hackers Reading Smart Starter Level 1	Hackers Reading Smart Starter Level 2	Hackers Reading Smart Level 1	Hackers Reading Smart Level 2	Hackers Reading Smart Level 3
				Hackers Reading Ground Level 1	Hackers Reading Ground Level 2
				Hackers Reading Path Level 1	Hackers Reading Path Level 2
					해커스 첫수능 영어 기초독해
듣기				해커스 중학영어듣기 모의고사 24회 Level 1	해커스 중학영어듣기 모의고사 24회 Level 2
어휘			해커스 3연타 중학영단어		
				해커스 보카 중학 기초	해커스 보카 중학 필수
					해커스 보카 중학 숙어

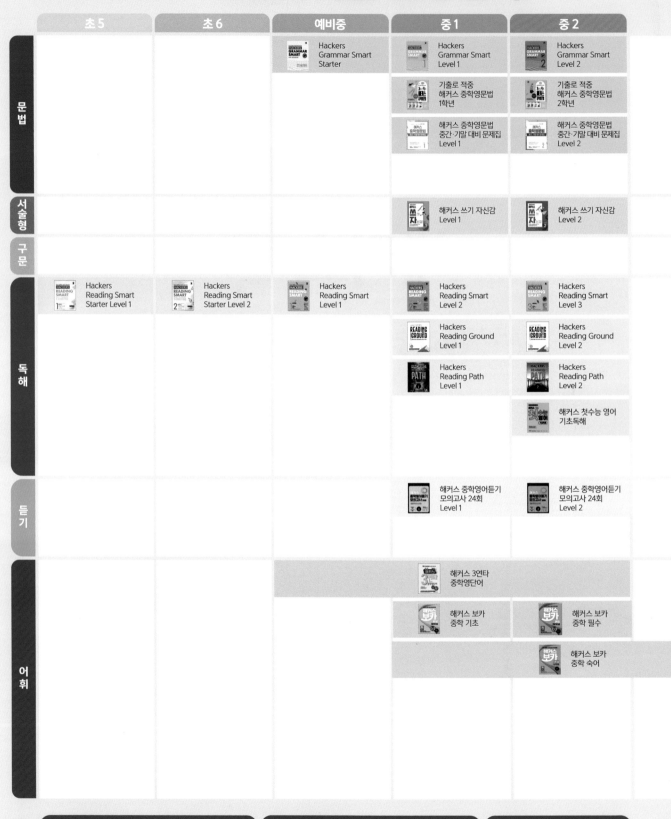

	READING	LISTENING	VOCA
토플	HACKERS APEX READING for the TOEFL iBT Basic/Intermediate/Advanced/Expert	HACKERS APEX LISTENING for the TOEFL iBT Basic/Intermediate/Advanced/Expert	HACKERS APEX VOCA for the TOEFL iBT HACKERS VOCABULARY

HACKERS GRAMMAR SMART STARTER

ANSWERS

HACKERS

UNIT 01 셀 수 있는 명사

Smart Check
p.12

1 O	2 X	3 O	4 X

Practice
p.13

A
1 a	2 an	3 a
4 an	5 a	6 an
7 a	8 a	9 an
10 a	11 an	12 a

B
1 birds	2 churches	3 thieves
4 parties	5 fish	6 potatoes
7 pens	8 cities	9 photos
10 feet	11 foxes	12 wishes

C
1 doll	2 wolves	3 map
4 boxes	5 orange	6 sheep
7 children	8 tomatoes	

UNIT 02 셀 수 없는 명사

Smart Check
p.14

1 X	2 X	3 O	4 X	5 O
6 X				

Practice
p.15

A
1 X	2 O	3 X
4 X	5 X	6 O
7 X	8 O	9 O
10 X		

B
1 money	2 honesty
3 Daniel	4 peace
5 bread	6 a glass of water

C
1 four bottles of juice
2 five pieces of paper
3 three bowls of rice
4 a glass of milk
5 two slices of pizza

Writing Exercise
p.16

A
1 three students
2 four cities
3 six men

---

4 an ant
5 two slices[pieces] of cheese
6 ten pianos
7 a week
8 five cookies
9 three pieces of paper

B
1 puppies	2 an owl
3 Friendship	4 an hour
5 a cup of coffee	6 Europe

C
1 an egg	2 a watermelon
3 milk	4 three peaches
5 bread	

D
1 three women
2 two candles
3 three knives
4 three dishes
5 a bottle of water
6 a glass of orange juice
7 two slices[pieces] of bread
8 four slices[pieces] of pizza

Chapter Test
p.18

1 ⑤	2 ①	3 ⑤	4 ④	5 ⑤	6 ③
7 potatoes		8 cups of tea		9 ②	10 ④
11 ⑤	12 ②	13 ②	14 ①		

15 watchs → watches   16 juices → juice
17 mice   18 money
19 two slices[pieces] of bread
20 two sheep, three children

1 ⑤ leaf – leaves

2 ① deer – deer

3 ⑤: 셀 수 있는 명사   ①②③④: 셀 수 없는 명사

4 ④ a → an

5 ⑤ a sugar → sugar

6 ③: an   ①②④⑤: a

7 빈칸 앞에 복수를 나타내는 ten(열, 십)이 있으므로 potato의 복수형 potatoes를 쓴다.

8 빈칸 앞에 복수를 나타내는 two(둘)가 있으므로 복수형을 쓰고, 셀 수 없는 명사(tea)의 복수형은 단위명사(cup)에 -(e)s를 붙여 만든다.

9 빈칸 앞에 a가 있으므로 셀 수 있는 명사의 복수형 notebooks는 쓸 수 없다.

10 빈칸 앞에 a(n)이 없으므로 셀 수 있는 명사의 단수형 Friend는 쓸 수 없다.

11 ⑤ babys → babies

12 ② coffees → coffee

13 • '식탁 위에 물 네 잔이 있다.'라는 의미이고 셀 수 없는 명사(water)의 복수형은 단위명사(glass)에 -(e)s를 붙여 만든다.
 • 빈칸 뒤에 첫소리가 모음으로 발음되는 셀 수 있는 명사(idea)가 있으므로 an을 쓴다.

14 • 도시의 고유한 이름을 나타내는 셀 수 없는 명사(Sydney) 앞에는 a(n)을 붙일 수 없다.
 • 빈칸 앞에 복수를 나타내는 five(다섯)가 있으므로 fish의 복수형 fish를 쓴다.

15 명사 watch의 복수형은 watches이다.

16 셀 수 없는 명사(juice)의 복수형은 단위명사(bottle)에 -(e)s를 붙여 만든다.

17 명사 mouse의 복수형은 mice이다.

18 셀 수 없는 명사(money)는 앞에 a(n)을 붙일 수 없고 복수형으로도 쓸 수 없다.

19 셀 수 없는 명사 bread는 단위명사 slice나 piece를 활용하여 수량을 나타내므로 two slices[pieces] of bread를 쓴다.

20 첫 번째 빈칸: sheep의 복수형은 sheep이므로 two sheep을 쓴다.
 두 번째 빈칸: child의 복수형은 children이므로 three children을 쓴다.

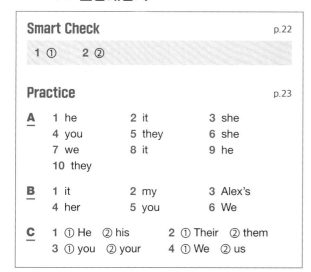

Chapter 02 | 대명사

UNIT 01 인칭대명사

Smart Check   p.22

1 ①   2 ②

Practice   p.23

A 1 he   2 it   3 she
 4 you   5 they   6 she
 7 we   8 it   9 he
 10 they

B 1 it   2 my   3 Alex's
 4 her   5 you   6 We

C 1 ① He ② his   2 ① Their ② them
 3 ① you ② your   4 ① We ② us

UNIT 02 this, that, it

Smart Check   p.24

1 ②   2 ②

Practice   p.25

A 1 That   2 These   3 It
 4 those   5 This

B 1 It   2 Those   3 These
 4 This   5 It   6 That

C 1 that   2 It   3 This
 4 These

Writing Exercise   p.26

A 1 her   2 Its   3 He
 4 it   5 Their   6 us
 7 They

B 1 Those   2 It   3 This
 4 These   5 That   6 It
 7 This   8 These

C 1 That is a maple tree
 2 These are old coins
 3 Her movie is popular
 4 This man is my soccer coach
 5 His new school uniform is comfortable
 6 Happiness is important to me

D 1 It   2 My
 3 These, them   4 Those, Their
 5 We

Chapter Test   p.28

1 ③   2 ④   3 ⑤   4 ②   5 We   6 his
7 ③   8 ⑤   9 ②   10 The teacher's
11 them   12 her   13 ③   14 ①   15 ③
16 It   17 Those   18 I, him
19 these → this

1 '아침 9시 30분이다.'라는 의미이므로 시간을 나타내는 비인칭 주어 It을 쓴다.

2 빈칸은 five children을 대신하는 주어 자리이므로 주격 인칭대명사 They를 쓴다.

3 빈칸 뒤에 소유의 대상이 되는 명사(jacket)가 있으므로 목적격 인칭대명사 him은 쓸 수 없다.

4 빈칸은 전치사 for의 목적어 자리이므로 소유격 인칭대명사 our는 쓸 수 없다.

5 Beth and I를 대신하는 주격 인칭대명사 We를 쓴다.

6 my brother's를 대신하는 소유격 인칭대명사 his를 쓴다.

7 ③ their → them

8　⑤ This → These

9　② This → It

10　빈칸 뒤에 소유의 대상이 되는 명사(chair)가 있으므로 소유격을 쓴다. 사람을 나타내는 명사(the teacher)의 소유격은 명사에 -'s를 붙여 만들므로 The teacher's를 쓴다.

11　빈칸은 cookies를 대신하는 동사 gives의 목적어 자리이므로 목적격 인칭대명사 them을 쓴다.

12　빈칸 뒤에 소유의 대상이 되는 명사(songs)가 있으므로 소유격 인칭대명사 her를 쓴다.

13　• '지금은 가을이다.'라는 의미이므로 계절을 나타내는 비인칭 주어 It을 쓴다.
　　• 빈칸은 a bicycle을 대신하는 주어 자리이므로 주격 인칭대명사 It을 쓴다.

14　'저쪽에 있는 저것은 너의 집이니?'라는 의미이므로 멀리 있는 사람이나 사물을 가리킬 때 쓰는 that(저 사람, 저것)을 쓴다.

15　③: 인칭대명사 it　①②④⑤: 비인칭 주어 it

16　날씨를 나타내는 비인칭 주어 It을 쓴다.

17　빈칸 뒤의 복수명사(blankets)를 꾸미는 복수형 Those(저 ~)를 쓴다.

18　첫 번째 빈칸: 주어 자리이므로 주격 인칭대명사 I를 쓴다.
　　두 번째 빈칸: 전치사 with의 목적어 자리이므로 목적격 인칭대명사 him을 쓴다.

19　단수명사(watermelon) 앞에는 단수형 this(이 ~)를 쓴다.

Chapter 03 ｜ be동사

UNIT 01 be동사의 현재형

Smart Check　　p.32

1 ①　　2 ②

Practice　　p.33

A　1 am　　2 is　　3 are
　　4 is　　5 are

B　1 He's　　2 You're　　3 They're
　　4 She's　　5 I'm　　6 We're
　　7 It's

C　1 am　　2 is　　3 are
　　4 is　　5 is　　6 are

UNIT 02 be동사 현재형의 부정문과 의문문

Smart Check　　p.34

1 ①　　2 ②

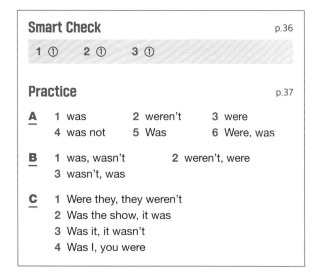

Practice　　p.35

A　1 I'm not　　2 is not　　3 Are
　　4 Is　　5 aren't　　6 isn't

B　1 I'm not
　　2 You're not[You aren't]
　　3 It's not[It isn't]
　　4 He's not[He isn't]
　　5 They're not[They aren't]

C　1 Is it, it isn't
　　2 Is he, he is
　　3 Is your sister, she isn't
　　4 Are the problems, they aren't
　　5 Are you and Edward, we are

UNIT 03 be동사의 과거형

Smart Check　　p.36

1 ①　　2 ①　　3 ①

Practice　　p.37

A　1 was　　2 weren't　　3 were
　　4 was not　　5 Was　　6 Were, was

B　1 was, wasn't　　2 weren't, were
　　3 wasn't, was

C　1 Were they, they weren't
　　2 Was the show, it was
　　3 Was it, it wasn't
　　4 Was I, you were

UNIT 04 There + be동사

Smart Check　　p.38

1 ①　　2 ①　　3 ②

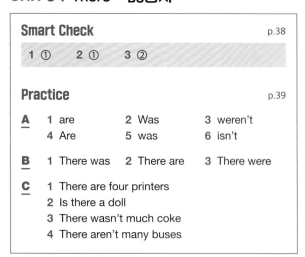

Practice　　p.39

A　1 are　　2 Was　　3 weren't
　　4 Are　　5 was　　6 isn't

B　1 There was　　2 There are　　3 There were

C　1 There are four printers
　　2 Is there a doll
　　3 There wasn't much coke
　　4 There aren't many buses

Writing Exercise
p.40

A
1 aren't   2 is   3 O
4 was   5 aren't   6 O

B
1 It is not[It's not/It isn't]
2 Was there
3 Jeffrey was not[wasn't]
4 We are not[We're not/We aren't]
5 There were
6 Are your friends
7 Ms. Green is

C
1 There are many fans
2 His book was not famous
3 Are you busy
4 Was there a tent
5 They were not Bill's sneakers

D
1 were thin   2 are fat
3 was short   4 is long
5 was a small TV   6 is a big TV

Chapter Test
p.42

1 ③   2 ②   3 ④   4 ⑤   5 ⑤   6 ②
7 ⑤   8 am   9 were not[weren't]
10 are not[aren't]   11 ①   12 ④   13 ④
14 Sam is not sleepy
15 Were those math problems difficult
16 My best friend is
17 There were apples
18 It was not[wasn't] cold

1 주어 We는 1인칭 복수이므로 are를 쓴다.

2 빈칸 뒤에 셀 수 없는 명사(juice)가 있으므로 is를 쓴다.

3 주어 Mariah는 3인칭 단수이고 과거를 나타내는 표현 (yesterday)이 있으므로 Is의 과거형 Was를 쓴다.

4 주어 Jack and Eric은 3인칭 복수이고 과거를 나타내는 표현(last week)이 있으므로 aren't의 과거형 weren't를 쓴다.

5 ⑤ I am not은 I'm not으로만 줄여 쓴다.

6 ② were → was

7 ⑤ are → were

8 나는 작년에 열두 살이었고 지금은 열세 살이라는 맥락이다. 주어 I는 1인칭 단수이므로 am을 쓴다.

9 한 시간 전에 오렌지 세 개가 아닌 다섯 개가 있었다는 맥락이다. 빈칸 뒤에 셀 수 있는 명사의 복수형(three oranges)이 있으므로 were not[weren't]를 쓴다.

10 Fred와 Natalie는 초등학생이 아닌 중학생이라는 맥락이다. 주어 They는 3인칭 복수이므로 are not[aren't]를 쓴다.

11 첫 번째 빈칸: 빈칸 뒤에 셀 수 있는 명사의 단수형(a wallet)이 있으므로 Is를 쓴다.
두 번째 빈칸: 「There + be동사」의 의문문에 대한 부정의 대답은 「No, there + be동사 + not.」의 형태이므로 isn't를 쓴다.

12 ④ you are → we are

13 ④: ~이다   ①②③⑤: (~에) 있다

14 be동사 현재형의 부정문: 「주어 + be동사의 현재형 + not」

15 be동사 과거형의 의문문: 「Was/Were + 주어 ~?」

16 주어 My best friend는 3인칭 단수이므로 is를 쓴다.

17 apples는 셀 수 있는 명사의 복수형이고 사과가 있었다고 했으므로 There were를 쓴다.

18 비인칭 주어 It은 3인칭 단수이고 춥지 않았다고 했으므로 was not[wasn't]를 쓴다.

Chapter 04 일반동사

UNIT 01 일반동사의 현재형

Smart Check
p.46
1 ①   2 ②

Practice
p.47

A
1 looks   2 hurries   3 finishes
4 learns   5 makes   6 passes
7 touches   8 runs   9 flies
10 stays   11 has   12 does

B
1 worries   2 eat   3 comes
4 teaches

C
1 practice   2 works   3 has

UNIT 02 일반동사 현재형의 부정문과 의문문

Smart Check
p.48
1 ②   2 ①

Practice
p.49

A
1 doesn't   2 don't   3 know
4 Do   5 sleep

B
1 We do not[don't] have
2 It does not[doesn't] rain
3 Clara does not[doesn't] watch
4 His parents do not[don't] exercise
5 Ms. Smith does not[doesn't] work
6 I do not[don't] take

<u>C</u> 1 Do, need, don't
    2 Do, speak, don't
    3 Does, look, does
    4 Does, ride, doesn't
    5 Do, want, do

UNIT 03 일반동사의 과거형

Smart Check   p.50

1 ②   2 ①

Practice   p.51

<u>A</u> 1 needed   2 liked   3 went
    4 tried   5 cut   6 used
    7 walked   8 planned   9 gave
    10 ate   11 watched   12 bought

<u>B</u> 1 ran   2 hit   3 studied
    4 met   5 stopped

<u>C</u> 1 saw   2 won   3 started

UNIT 04 일반동사 과거형의 부정문과 의문문

Smart Check   p.52

1 ②   2 ②

Practice   p.53

<u>A</u> 1 didn't   2 stay   3 Did
    4 didn't   5 borrow

<u>B</u> 1 He did not[didn't] fail
    2 Angela did not[didn't] make
    3 I did not[didn't] get
    4 The woman did not[didn't] find
    5 Ms. Green did not[didn't] cut

<u>C</u> 1 Did, invite, did   2 Did, give, didn't
    3 Did, go, did   4 Did, visit, didn't
    5 Did, arrive, did

Writing Exercise   p.54

<u>A</u> 1 Tony chatted
    2 I do not[don't] study
    3 Did she learn
    4 His uncle goes
    5 Does Janet like
    6 They did not[didn't] put

<u>B</u> 1 I heard the bad news
    2 Did my dog bark
    3 Do you have an English class
    4 Terry did not write a letter
    5 Megan and I climb mountains
    6 The student does not remember

<u>C</u> ⓐ moved   ⓑ live   ⓒ works
    ⓓ taught   ⓔ makes   ⓕ tries
    ⓖ passed

<u>D</u> 1 Does Martha take
    2 Did Ken and Ian play
    3 Do you use
    4 Did the puppies sleep

Chapter Test   p.56

1 ⑤   2 ④   3 ⑤   4 ①   5 ④
6 they do   7 it didn't   8 ③   9 ②
10 ⑤   11 ③, ⑤   12 found → find
13 heard the news   14 walks his dog
15 Did you lock the door
16 Ollie does not like summer
17 Do they live in New York
18 My friends did not break the window

1 ⑤ wash – washes

2 ④ play – played

3 빈칸 뒤에 동사의 3인칭 단수 현재형(works)이 있으므로 3인칭 단수 주어 Mr. Scott을 쓴다.

4 주어 We는 1인칭 복수이므로 climb를 쓴다. 부정형은 don't climb이다.

5 과거를 나타내는 표현(last month)이 있으므로 didn't go를 쓴다.

6 주어 they는 3인칭 복수이므로 일반동사 현재형의 의문문에 대한 긍정의 대답 Yes, they do를 쓴다.

7 주어 the accident는 3인칭 단수이므로 일반동사 과거형의 의문문에 대한 부정의 대답 No, it didn't를 쓴다.

8 ③ buys → bought

9 ② Does → Do

10 • 과거를 나타내는 표현(yesterday)이 있으므로 동사 write의 과거형 wrote을 쓴다.
    • 주어 The boys는 3인칭 복수이므로 don't play를 쓴다.

11 ③ did → does
    ⑤ he does → we do

12 일반동사 과거형의 의문문: 「Did + 주어 + 동사원형 ~?」

13 동사 hear의 과거형: heard

14 주어 Dennis는 3인칭 단수이므로 walks를 쓴다.

15 일반동사 과거형의 의문문: 「Did + 주어 + 동사원형 ~?」

16 일반동사 현재형의 부정문: 「주어 + do/does not + 동사원형」

17 일반동사 현재형의 의문문: 「Do/Does + 주어 + 동사원형 ~?」

18 일반동사 과거형의 부정문: 「주어 + did not[didn't] + 동사원형」

Chapter 05 | 형용사와 부사

UNIT 01 형용사

Smart Check   p.60

1 ②   2 ①

Practice   p.61

A
1 yellow   2 tired   3 hot
4 round   5 cloudy   6 curly

B
1 tall tree   2 salty   3 much
4 something scary

C
1 some   2 many   3 any
4 much

UNIT 02 부사

Smart Check   p.62

1 speaks   2 small
3 I finished my homework   4 quickly

Practice   p.63

A
1 softly   2 heavily   3 fast
4 possibly   5 wisely   6 early
7 quietly   8 clearly   9 noisily
10 horribly

B
1 Sadly   2 is often   3 well
4 perfectly   5 sometimes exercise

C
1 often   2 seldom   3 usually
4 never   5 always

Writing Exercise   p.64

A
1 many visitors   2 loudly
3 sometimes takes   4 any homework

5 hard   6 much snow

B
1 looks handsome
2 gives much love
3 is really hungry
4 wanted something spicy
5 are often busy
6 baked some chocolate cookies

C
1 bright   2 beautifully
3 cold   4 high

D
1 often plays tennis
2 always eats breakfast
3 is never late for school
4 seldom reads a book
5 sometimes takes a piano lesson

Chapter Test   p.66

1 ③   2 ⑤   3 ①   4 ⑤   5 ④   6 ④
7 ①   8 ③   9 ④   10 ②   11 late
12 many → much   13 any → some
14 fastly → fast   15 easily → easy
16 Miranda wanted something special

1 동사(are) 뒤에서 주어(Emperor penguins)를 보충 설명하는 형용사가 필요하므로 부사 slowly는 쓸 수 없다.

2 빈칸 뒤에 명사(student)가 있으므로 동사, 형용사, 다른 부사, 문장 전체를 꾸미는 부사 quietly는 쓸 수 없다.

3 동사(talked)를 꾸미는 부사가 필요하므로 형용사 friendly는 쓸 수 없다.

4 • '나는 몇 권의 과학책을 샀다.'라는 의미의 긍정문이므로 some을 쓴다.
  • '냉장고 안에 양파가 좀 있니?'라는 의미의 의문문이므로 any를 쓴다. onions는 셀 수 있는 명사의 복수형이므로 셀 수 없는 명사 앞에 쓰는 much는 쓸 수 없다.

5 • 빈칸 뒤에 셀 수 없는 명사(salt)가 있으므로 much를 쓴다.
  • 빈칸 뒤에 셀 수 있는 명사의 복수형(questions)이 있으므로 many를 쓴다. 부정문이므로 주로 긍정문에 쓰는 some은 쓸 수 없다.

6 ④: 형용사   ①②③⑤: 부사

7 빈도부사(always)는 일반동사(have) 앞에 온다.

8 빈도부사(usually)는 be동사(are) 뒤에 온다.

9 ④ some → any

10 ② greatly → great

11 'Sarah는 학교에 늦게 왔다.'라는 의미이므로 동사(came)를 꾸미는 부사 late(늦게)를 쓴다.

12 money는 셀 수 없는 명사이므로 much를 쓴다.

13 '그는 한 시간 전에 약간의 약을 먹었다.'라는 의미의 긍정문
이므로 some을 쓴다.

14 '얼룩말들은 정말 빠르게 달린다.'라는 의미이므로 동사
(run)를 꾸미는 부사 fast(빠르게)를 쓴다.

15 '그 영어 시험은 아주 쉬웠다.'라는 의미이므로 동사(was)
뒤에서 주어(The English test)를 보충 설명하는 형용사
easy를 쓴다.

16 -thing으로 끝나는 대명사(something)를 꾸밀 때는 형용
사(special)가 대명사 뒤에 온다.

Chapter 06 | 현재진행시제와 미래시제

UNIT 01 현재진행시제

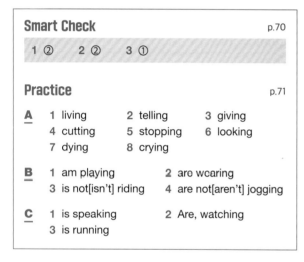

Smart Check p.70

1 ②   2 ②   3 ①

Practice p.71

A
1 living   2 telling   3 giving
4 cutting   5 stopping   6 looking
7 dying   8 crying

B
1 am playing   2 are wearing
3 is not[isn't] riding   4 are not[aren't] jogging

C
1 is speaking   2 Are, watching
3 is running

UNIT 02 미래시제

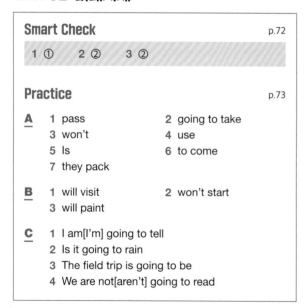

Smart Check p.72

1 ①   2 ②   3 ②

Practice p.73

A
1 pass   2 going to take
3 won't   4 use
5 Is   6 to come
7 they pack

B
1 will visit   2 won't start
3 will paint

C
1 I am[I'm] going to tell
2 Is it going to rain
3 The field trip is going to be
4 We are not[aren't] going to read

Writing Exercise p.74

A
1 won't keep   2 am going to order
3 is not sitting   4 Is, hiding
5 Are, going to invite   6 Will, be
7 are walking

B
1 They are not doing
2 Will you apologize
3 The girls are not going to take
4 The mall will not open
5 Are you and your friend cooking

C
1 she isn't, She is[She's] washing
2 Is Mr. Brown working, he isn't
3 Are the students sitting, they are
4 he isn't, He is[He's] fixing

D
ⓐ am going to read
ⓑ are going to travel
ⓒ Will, visit
ⓓ is going to make
ⓔ will watch

Chapter Test p.76

1 ④   2 ③   3 ①   4 ②   5 ①, ③ 6 ⑤
7 we are   8 she isn't   9 ⑤   10 ②
11 ③   12 ④   13 It will not rain
14 Is she making
15 They are not going to take
16 Is Anna going to stay
17 I am not thinking
18 Will you sell your bicycle

1 ④ run – runinng

2 ③ give – giving

3 tomorrow가 있으므로 미래시제 will return의 will을 쓴다.

4 주어 the kids는 3인칭 복수이므로 지금(now) 진행되고 있
는 동작을 나타내는 현재진행시제 Are ~ playing의 Are를
쓴다.

5 미래시제 are going to eat이 쓰였으므로 과거시제와 주로
함께 쓰이는 부사(구) yesterday와 last night은 쓸 수 없다.

6 ⑤: is   ①②③④: are

7 미래시제 Are ~ going to visit으로 묻고 있으므로 be
going to가 있는 미래시제의 의문문에 대한 긍정의 대답
Yes, we are를 쓴다.

8 현재진행시제 Is ~ planting으로 묻고 있으므로 현재진행시
제의 의문문에 대한 부정의 대답 No, she isn't를 쓴다.

9 ⑤ not are cleaning → are not[aren't] cleaning

10　② won't listens → won't listen

11　• 주어 you는 2인칭이고 빈칸 뒤에 be going to가 있는 미래시제의 의문문(「be동사 + 주어 + going to + 동사원형 ~?」)을 만드는 you going to drink가 있으므로 be동사 Are를 쓴다.
　　• 주어 The students는 3인칭 복수이고 빈칸 뒤에 동사의 V-ing형(singing)이 있으므로 「be동사의 현재형 + V-ing」 형태의 현재진행시제를 만드는 be동사 are를 쓴다.

12　• Fred는 지금 벤치에 앉아 있는 것이 아니라 경주로에서 조깅하고 있다는 맥락이므로 is not을 쓴다.
　　• 빈칸 앞에 be동사(are)가 있으므로 「be동사의 현재형 + V-ing」 형태의 현재진행시제를 만드는 feeding을 쓴다.

13　will이 있는 미래시제의 부정문: 「주어 + will not + 동사원형」

14　주어 she는 3인칭 단수이므로 현재진행시제의 의문문 Is she making ~?을 쓴다.

15　주어 They는 3인칭 복수이므로 be going to가 있는 미래시제의 부정문 They are not going to take를 쓴다.

16　be going to가 있는 미래시제의 의문문: 「be동사 + 주어 + going to + 동사원형 ~?」

17　현재진행시제의 부정문: 「주어 + be동사의 현재형 + not + V-ing」

18　will이 있는 미래시제의 의문문: 「Will + 주어 + 동사원형 ~?」

Chapter 07 | 조동사

UNIT 01 can, may

Smart Check　　p.80

1 말할 수 있다　　2 닫아도 되니
3 가도 된다　　4 슬플지도 모른다

Practice　　p.81

A　1 stay　　2 can　　3 be
　　4 may return　　5 cannot　　6 I see
　　7 Can

B　1 cannot　　2 may　　3 can

C　1 may snow　　2 can use　　3 cannot ski

UNIT 02 must, have to

Smart Check　　p.82

1 일어나야 한다　　2 앉으면 안 된다
3 기다려야 한다　　4 살 필요가 없다

Practice　　p.83

A　1 show　　2 have to
　　3 must not　　4 has
　　5 doesn't　　6 don't have to

B　1 must not ride　　2 must wash
　　3 must not talk

C　1 have to take
　　2 don't have to worry
　　3 has to walk
　　4 doesn't have to prepare

Writing Exercise　　p.84

A　1 must　　2 say
　　3 you run　　4 doesn't have to
　　5 drink　　6 cannot[can't]
　　7 don't have to

B　1 must not fish　　2 has to find
　　3 Can[May], put　　4 may be
　　5 can[may] turn　　6 must listen

C　1 You don't have to wear a tie
　　2 Alan must return the book
　　3 May I borrow your cell phone
　　4 Can you use chopsticks
　　5 Megan and I have to clean the table
　　6 His uncle can speak three languages

D　1 cannot[can't] reach　　2 must not run
　　3 may be　　4 don't have to water

Chapter Test　　p.86

1 ①　　2 ③　　3 ④　　4 ③　　5 ④　　6 may
7 don't have to　　8 must not　　9 ②　　10 ①
11 ③　　12 ④　　13 comes → come
14 not must → must not
15 may be true
16 must[have to] take a shower
17 cannot[can't] solve this math problem
18 must not use plastics

1　'나는 스페인어를 말할 수 있다. 나는 2년 동안 그것을 공부했다.'라는 의미이므로 can(~할 수 있다)을 쓴다.

2　'Maria는 부엌에 있을지도 모른다. 그녀는 5분 전에 요리하고 있었다.'라는 의미이므로 may(~일지도 모른다)를 쓴다.

3　'너는 그 프라이팬을 만지면 안 된다. 그것은 뜨겁다.'라는 의미이므로 must not(~하면 안 된다)을 쓴다.

4 '우리는 서둘러야 한다. 그 수업은 곧 시작할 것이다.'라는 의미이므로 have to(~해야 한다)를 쓴다.

5 ④: 허가(~해도 된다) ①②③⑤: 능력·가능(~할 수 있다)

6 '너는 나의 스웨터를 가져도 된다. 그것은 나에게 너무 작다.'라는 의미이므로 may(~해도 된다)를 쓴다.

7 '나는 오늘 일찍 잠자리에 들 필요가 없다. 내일은 일요일이다.'라는 의미이므로 don't have to(~할 필요가 없다)를 쓴다.

8 '우리는 길을 건너면 안 된다. 신호등이 빨간색이다.'라는 의미이므로 must not(~하면 안 된다)을 쓴다.

9 첫 번째 빈칸: '내가 이 컵을 사용해도 되니?'라는 의미이므로 '~해도 된다'라는 의미의 May나 Can을 쓴다.
두 번째 빈칸: '하지만 너는 우선 그것을 씻어야 한다. 그것은 더럽다.'라는 의미이므로 have to(~해야 한다)를 쓴다.

10 첫 번째 빈칸: '나는 나의 기차표를 사야 해.'라는 의미이므로 '~해야 한다'라는 의미의 must나 have to를 쓴다.
두 번째 빈칸: 내가 이미 그것을 사서 너는 살 필요가 없다는 맥락이므로 don't have to(~할 필요가 없다)를 쓴다.

11 ③ can rides → can ride

12 ④ don't have to take → doesn't have to take

13 「조동사 + 동사원형」

14 must의 부정형: must not

15 추측(~일지도 모른다)을 나타내는 may를 쓴다.

16 주어 You는 2인칭 단수이므로 의무(~해야 한다)를 나타내는 must나 have to를 쓴다.

17 '~할 수 없다'라는 의미의 cannot[can't]를 쓴다.

18 강한 금지(~하면 안 된다)를 나타내는 must not을 쓴다.

Chapter 08 | 동사의 종류

UNIT 01 감각동사

Smart Check
p.90

1 ① 2 ② 3 ②

Practice
p.91

A 1 great 2 sounds 3 friendly
    4 taste 5 good 6 smelled like

B 1 feels 2 tastes 3 looks like
    4 sounds

C 1 smells terrible
    2 tastes like an orange
    3 looks peaceful

UNIT 02 수여동사

Smart Check
p.92

1 ② 2 ②

Practice
p.93

A 1 간접 목적어: Alice, 직접 목적어: an e-mail
    2 간접 목적어: them, 직접 목적어: napkins
    3 간접 목적어: her classmate,
      직접 목적어: textbooks
    4 간접 목적어: me, 직접 목적어: the lunch box
    5 간접 목적어: his girlfriend,
      직접 목적어: a teddy bear

B 1 taught 2 asked 3 showed
    4 wrote 5 cooked

C 1 reads me a fairy tale
    2 gave presents to the kids
    3 built his brother a sandcastle

Writing Exercise
p.94

A 1 tastes bitter
    2 passed her the sauce
    3 showed our house to the neighbors
    4 looks clean
    5 smells like medicine
    6 got a glass of water for me

B 1 feels warm
    2 asked me a question
    3 looks like a turtle
    4 sounded loud
    5 built a garden for us
    6 sent him an e-mail

C 1 lent 2 feels 3 wrote
    4 bought 5 sounds like

D 1 sounded sad
    2 gave Sally an award
    3 looked like sheep
    4 made gloves for her son

Chapter Test
p.96

1 ②, ⑤ 2 ②, ③ 3 ①, ⑤
4 felt 5 lent 6 tasted 7 ④
8 ③ 9 ④ 10 ③ 11 ④ 12 ①, ⑤
13 looks exciting

14 told his friend a secret

15 passed the paper to me

16 felt tired

17 found her a shoe

1 감각동사(smells)의 주격 보어 자리에는 형용사만 오므로 부사 wonderfully와 명사 flowers는 쓸 수 없다.

2 빈칸 뒤에 간접 목적어(us)와 직접 목적어(lunch)가 있으므로 수여동사가 아닌 feel과 look은 쓸 수 없다.

3 빈칸 뒤에 형용사 주격 보어(sour)가 있으므로 감각동사가 아닌 makes와 shows는 쓸 수 없다.

4 빈칸 뒤에 형용사 주격 보어(hungry)가 있고 'Peter는 아침에 배고프게 느꼈다.'라는 의미이므로 감각동사 felt를 쓴다.

5 빈칸 뒤에 간접 목적어(her sister)와 직접 목적어(a red jacket)가 있으므로 수여동사 lent를 쓴다.

6 빈칸 뒤에 「like + 명사(chocolate)」가 있고 '그 케이크는 초콜릿 같은 맛이 났다.'라는 의미이므로 감각동사 tasted를 쓴다.

7 ④ sounded angrily → sounded angry

8 ③ told a story me → told a story to me[told me a story]

9 ④ looked a doctor → looked like a doctor

10 첫 번째 빈칸: 빈칸 뒤에 간접 목적어(me)와 직접 목적어(a gift)가 있고 'Ricky가 나에게 선물을 줬어.'라는 의미이므로 수여동사 gave를 쓴다.
두 번째 빈칸: 감각동사(looks)의 주격 보어 자리에는 형용사만 오므로 형용사 heavy를 쓴다.

11 첫 번째 빈칸: 빈칸 뒤에 명사(butter)가 있고 '그 팬케이크들은 버터 같은 냄새가 난다.'라는 의미이므로 smell like를 쓴다.
두 번째 빈칸: 「make + 직접 목적어 + for + 간접 목적어」

12 ①⑤: 「감각동사 + like + 명사」

13 「look + 형용사」: ~하게 보이다

14 「tell + 간접 목적어 + 직접 목적어」

15 「pass + 직접 목적어 + to + 간접 목적어」

16 「feel + 형용사」: ~하게 느끼다

17 「find + 간접 목적어 + 직접 목적어」

Chapter 09 | 전치사

UNIT 01 장소를 나타내는 전치사

Smart Check p.100

1 ②   2 ②

Practice p.101

A 1 on   2 us   3 in
4 next to   5 at

B 1 on   2 behind   3 in front of
4 in   5 under

C 1 in front of   2 in   3 next to
4 under   5 at

UNIT 02 시간을 나타내는 전치사

Smart Check p.102

1 ②   2 ①

Practice p.103

A 1 at   2 on   3 in
4 on   5 in   6 in
7 on   8 at   9 in
10 at

B 1 during   2 after   3 before
4 for   5 in   6 on

C 1 at   2 for   3 before
4 after   5 during

Writing Exercise p.104

A 1 behind   2 at   3 under
4 in   5 after   6 on

B 1 at 11:30
2 in front of the mirror
3 for 30 minutes
4 on the roof
5 in Canada
6 during the weekend

C 1 in   2 behind   3 under
4 next to   5 on

D 1 in the morning
2 after breakfast
3 before the violin lesson
4 for an hour

Chapter Test p.106

1 ②   2 ③   3 ①   4 ④   5 ③
6 in front of   7 after   8 before   9 ①

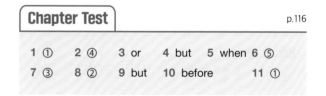

10 ⑤　　11 ④　　12 ①　　13 ④

14 behind the cloud

15 on Thursday

16 under the bed

17 is an old tree in the forest

18 brush my teeth after lunch

1　전치사(next to) 뒤에 인칭대명사가 올 때는 목적격을 쓰므로 주격 인칭대명사 I는 쓸 수 없다.

2　도시(Paris)를 나타낼 때는 전치사 in(~ 안에, ~에)을 쓴다.

3　시각(8 o'clock)을 나타낼 때는 전치사 at(~에)을 쓴다.

4　'그 영화는 두 시간 동안 상영했다.'라는 의미이고 two hours는 숫자를 포함한 기간 표현이므로 전치사 for(~ 동안)를 쓴다.

5　• 표면(the table)에 접촉하여 위에 있는 상태를 나타낼 때는 전치사 on(~ 위에, ~에)을 쓴다.
　　• 기념일(her birthday)을 나타낼 때는 전치사 on(~에)을 쓴다.

6　'~ 앞에'라는 의미의 전치사 in front of를 쓴다.

7　월요일에 요가 수업이 테니스 수업 후에 시작하므로 전치사 after(~ 후에)를 쓴다.

8　금요일에는 골프 수업 전에 수업이 없으므로 전치사 before(~ 전에)를 쓴다.

9　하나의 지점(the bus stop)을 나타낼 때는 '~에, ~에서'라는 의미의 전치사 at을 쓴다.

10　⑤: in　①②③④: at

11　④: during　①②③⑤: for

12　① next → next to

13　④ at → in

14　'~ 뒤에'라는 의미의 전치사 behind를 쓴다.

15　요일(Thursday)을 나타낼 때는 '~에'라는 의미의 전치사 on을 쓴다.

16　'~ 아래에'라는 의미의 전치사 under를 쓴다.

17　비교적 넓은 장소(forest)를 나타낼 때는 '~ 안에, ~에'라는 의미의 전치사 in을 쓴다.

18　'~ 후에'라는 의미의 전치사 after를 쓴다.

Chapter 10 | 접속사

UNIT 01 and, but, or

Smart Check
p.110

1 ①　　2 ①　　3 ②

Practice
p.111

A　1 but　　2 and　　3 or
　　4 but　　5 and

B　1 but　　2 and　　3 or
　　4 and　　5 or　　6 but

C　1 or　　2 and　　3 but

UNIT 02 when, before, after, because

Smart Check
p.112

1 ②　　2 ②　　3 ①

Practice
p.113

A　1 after　　2 because　　3 when
　　4 do　　5 Before

B　1 when　　2 before　　3 When
　　4 after

C　1 when　　2 before　　3 After
　　4 because

Writing Exercise
p.114

A　1 when I got
　　2 but they did not[didn't] believe
　　3 after he ate
　　4 Because he is not[isn't]
　　5 before you enter
　　6 carrots, onions, and pumpkins

B　1 borrow novels or comic books
　　2 before the game begins
　　3 after she played
　　4 and she teaches art
　　5 Because Joe needed new pants
　　6 but the server brought pepper

C　1 or　　2 because　　3 and
　　4 When　　5 but

D　1 and　　2 after　　3 Before
　　4 when　　5 because　　6 but

Chapter Test
p.116

1 ①　　2 ④　　3 or　　4 but　　5 when　6 ⑤
7 ③　　8 ②　　9 but　　10 before　　11 ①

12 ②   13 because he was sick

14 when I have free time

15 after they played with sand

16 will eat → eats

---

1 '나는 저녁 식사로 피자와 파스타를 먹었다.'라는 의미이므로 and(~과, 그리고)를 쓴다.

2 '너무 추웠기 때문에 Jerry는 스카프를 했다.'라는 의미이므로 because(~하기 때문에)를 쓴다.

3 '우리는 오늘 박물관이나 서점에 갈 것이다.'라는 의미이므로 or(또는, ~이거나, 아니면)를 쓴다.

4 '나는 우유를 좋아하지 않지만, 치즈는 좋아한다.'라는 의미이므로 but(하지만, 그러나)을 쓴다.

5 '선생님이 도착하셨을 때 종이 울렸다.'라는 의미이므로 when(~할 때)을 쓴다.

6 ⑤: when   ①②③④: because

7 · '펭귄은 날개가 있지만, 날 수 없다.'라는 의미이므로 but(하지만, 그러나)을 쓴다.
   · '나는 코미디를 좋아하기 때문에 저 영화를 볼 것이다.'라는 의미이므로 because(~하기 때문에)를 쓴다.

8 · '그녀는 런던에 사니, 아니면 뉴욕에 사니?'라는 의미이므로 or(또는, ~이거나, 아니면)를 쓴다.
   · 'Owen은 비가 그친 후에 무지개를 봤다.'라는 의미이므로 after(~한 후에)를 쓴다.

9 · 'Jane은 돼지고기를 먹지 않지만, 소고기는 먹는다.'라는 의미이므로 but(하지만, 그러나)을 쓴다.
   · '수학은 어렵지만 흥미롭다.'라는 의미이므로 but(하지만, 그러나)을 쓴다.

10 · '엄마는 냄비에 감자를 넣기 전에 물을 끓이셨다.'라는 의미이므로 before(~하기 전에)를 쓴다.
   · 'Marie는 잠이 들기 전에 나에게 문자 메시지를 보냈다.'라는 의미이므로 before(~하기 전에)를 쓴다.

11 ① or → but

12 ② Because → When

13 '~하기 때문에'라는 의미의 because를 쓴다.

14 '~할 때'라는 의미의 when을 쓴다. 시간을 나타내는 절(when ~ time)에서는 미래시제 대신 현재시제를 쓰고 주어 I는 1인칭 단수이므로 have를 쓴다.

15 '~한 후에'라는 의미의 after를 쓴다.

16 시간을 나타내는 절(before ~ dinner)에서는 미래시제 대신 현재시제를 쓰고 주어 she는 3인칭 단수이므로 eats를 쓴다.

UNIT 01   의문사 의문문 I

Smart Check   p.120

1 ①   2 ②   3 ②   4 ①

Practice   p.121

A   1 Who   2 What   3 Whose
    4 Who   5 What   6 What
    7 Whom

B   1 ⓓ   2 ⓐ   3 ⓑ
    4 ⓒ

C   1 Who   2 What   3 Whose
    4 Who

UNIT 02   의문사 의문문 II

Smart Check   p.122

1 ①   2 ②   3 ①   4 ②

Practice   p.123

A   1 Where   2 Why   3 How
    4 When   5 long

B   1 ⓓ   2 ⓒ   3 ⓐ
    4 ⓑ

C   1 How often   2 How tall
    3 How many   4 How old

UNIT 03   명령문, 청유문, 감탄문

Smart Check   p.124

1 ①   2 ②

Practice   p.125

A   1 What   2 Turn   3 How
    4 Don't   5 Let's   6 those are

B   1 Don't talk   2 Let's cross
    3 Call   4 Let's not waste
    5 Help

C   1 What nice cars   2 How high
    3 How brave

Writing Exercise

p.126

A
1 When   2 Where   3 Who
4 What   5 Let's wait
6 Take   7 Don't[Do not] lie
8 Let's not enter

B
1 How clear   2 Let's not eat
3 What a smart boy   4 Be polite
5 Whose socks   6 How many visitors

C
1 How long   2 What   3 Who
4 Where   5 Why   6 When
7 How old

D
1 Don't[Do not] feed   2 What a huge waterfall
3 Eat   4 How strongly

Chapter Test

p.128

1 ③   2 ④   3 Whose   4 What
5 Why 6 ⑤   7 ④   8 ②
9 Why → How   10 ②   11 ①
12 How long did we wait
13 What a clean room this is
14 Who(m) will they meet
15 Where did you buy this hat
16 Let's not order pizza
17 Don't[Do not] take pictures

1 긍정 청유문: 「Let's + 동사원형」

2 How 감탄문: 「How + 형용사/부사 + (주어 + 동사)!」

3 '그것은 Kate의 재킷이야.'라고 대답했으므로 '누구의'라는 의미의 형용사로 쓰여 명사 앞에서 명사를 꾸밀 수 있는 Whose를 쓴다.

4 '나는 테니스를 배울 거야.'라고 대답했으므로 사물에 대해 물을 때 쓰는 What(무엇이, 무엇을)을 쓴다.

5 '왜냐하면 그녀의 책은 흥미롭기 때문이야.'라고 대답했으므로 이유를 물을 때 쓰는 Why(왜)를 쓴다.

6 ⑤ watch not → not watch

7 ④ How an → How

8 첫 번째 빈칸: '그것은 나의 도마뱀이야.'라고 대답했으므로 동물에 대해 물을 때 쓰는 What(무엇이, 무엇을)을 쓴다.
두 번째 빈칸: What 감탄문은 「What + (a/an) + 형용사 + 명사 + (주어 + 동사)!」의 형태이다.

9 '지하철 2호선을 타라.'라고 대답했으므로 방법을 물을 때 쓰는 How(어떻게)를 쓴다.

10 ② Where(어디에(서))로 묻고 있으므로 장소에 해당하는 것으로 대답한다.

11 첫 번째 빈칸: '왜냐하면 Maria가 창문을 깼기 때문이야.'라

12 기간을 묻고 있으므로 How long을 쓴다.

13 What 감탄문: 「What + (a/an) + 형용사 + 명사 + (주어 + 동사)!」

14 '누구를'을 의미하는 Who(m)을 쓴다.

15 '어디에(서)'를 의미하는 Where를 쓴다.

16 부정 청유문: 「Let's not + 동사원형」

17 부정 명령문: 「Don't[Do not] + 동사원형」

Chapter 01 명사

UNIT 01 셀 수 있는 명사

p.2

A 1 a   2 pigs   3 photos
  4 leaves   5 deer

B 1 an idea   2 a watch   3 An elephant
  4 a scientist   5 a university

C 1 a carrot   2 two chairs   3 an umbrella
  4 five buses   5 four teeth

D 1 an apple   2 three men   3 five classes
  4 seven toys

UNIT 02 셀 수 없는 명사

p.3

A 1 an   2 X   3 X
  4 a   5 X

B 1 bowls of soup   2 California
  3 help   4 pieces
  5 coffee

C 1 salt   2 slices of cake
  3 Amy   4 glasses of milk

D 1 two bottles of water   2 Jejudo
  3 ten pieces of paper   4 happiness

Writing Exercise ✚

p.4

A 1 air   2 a uniform
  3 kindness   4 an orange
  5 an apple pie   6 Europe
  7 a blue umbrella

B 1 three buses   2 seven children
  3 five cups of tea   4 four stories
  5 four bowls of soup   6 six watches
  7 two fish   8 ten men

C 1 hope   2 two feet   3 money
  4 cheese   5 an elementary school
  6 a glass of milk

D 1 makes chocolate cookies
  2 eats five pieces of pizza
  3 is in New York
  4 watch a movie
  5 needs two slices of bread
  6 drinks four bottles of water

Chapter 02 대명사

UNIT 01 인칭대명사

p.6

A 1 its   2 me   3 your
  4 They

B 1 his   2 She   3 us
  4 them

C 1 my   2 her   3 Kevin's
  4 Our   5 you

D 1 her   2 them   3 Your
  4 us   5 Mark's

UNIT 02 this, that, it

p.7

A 1 Those   2 It   3 that
  4 these

B 1 It   2 These   3 This
  4 Those   5 It   6 That

C 1 Those buildings   2 This T-shirt
  3 These bananas

D 1 These are my family members
  2 Terry lives in that apartment
  3 It is 100 meters

Writing Exercise ✚

p.8

A 1 It   2 them   3 his
  4 Her   5 her   6 We

B 1 your   2 It   3 They
  4 This   5 These   6 me
  7 That   8 His

C 1 their plan   2 It is Monday
  3 My eyes   4 Those cows
  5 These are math textbooks
  6 That is a new library

D 1 This is my book report
  2 His mom makes dinner
  3 That train goes to the airport
  4 Our parents think about us
  5 Those kittens drink milk
  6 It is two kilometers

Chapter 03 be동사

UNIT 01 be동사의 현재형

A p.10
1 is 2 am 3 are
4 is 5 are

B
1 is 2 am 3 is
4 are 5 are

C
1 They're my classmates
2 We're at the flower shop
3 I'm tired today
4 She's on the boat
5 It's Emily's laptop

D
1 Their stories are 2 Kelly is
3 We are[We're] 4 The man is

UNIT 02 be동사 현재형의 부정문과 의문문

A p.11
1 aren't 2 Are 3 isn't
4 I am

B
1 He's not[He isn't] 2 This question isn't
3 I'm not 4 Chris and I aren't

C
1 Is New York, it is 2 Is Samuel, he isn't
3 Are you and your brother, we are

D
1 Mr. Wilson isn't 2 Those boys aren't
3 Are these oranges 4 Is the scarf

UNIT 03 be동사의 과거형

A p.12
1 were 2 was 3 wasn't
4 Were, weren't

B
1 Alex wasn't 2 These pictures weren't
3 They weren't 4 The sunlight wasn't

C
1 Was the musical, it wasn't
2 Were these singers, they weren't
3 Was George, he was

D
1 They were not[weren't] at the museum
2 Was Scott with you
3 The box was empty
4 Were those women basketball players

UNIT 04 There + be동사

A p.13
1 is 2 Are 3 weren't
4 was

B
1 There isn't enough money
2 Are there five floors
3 There weren't many trees
4 Was there a bus stop

C
1 There is a soccer match
2 Are there 20 students
3 There were two air conditioners

D
1 Was there a flag
2 There are not[aren't] any notebooks
3 Are there five spoons
4 There were many children

Writing Exercise ✚

A p.14
1 Are 2 was 3 were
4 Is 5 aren't 6 wasn't
7 isn't 8 weren't

B
1 Are you and Silvia, we aren't
2 Were Henry and Jerry, they were
3 Is your brother, he is
4 Was Ms. Davis, she wasn't
5 Were the apples, they weren't

C
1 Are you thirsty
2 The math test was not[wasn't] easy
3 There is a gym
4 We were not[weren't] tired
5 Is he twelve years old
6 Lisa was in the swimming pool

D
1 My answer was not wrong
2 This jacket was on sale
3 Are your hands clean
4 Paul's house is on the mountain
5 There were not many people
6 Was there an old bookstore

일반동사

UNIT 01 일반동사의 현재형

p.16

A
1 misses 2 cries 3 has
4 goes 5 buy

B
1 jumps 2 brushes 3 get
4 carries

C
1 study hard for the test
2 listens to the radio in the evening
3 clean the room on weekends

D
1 This plant needs
2 His sister does
3 Cindy washes
4 Those students wear

UNIT 02 일반동사 현재형의 부정문과 의문문

p.17

A
1 Do 2 live 3 don't
4 Does 5 doesn't

B
1 does not[doesn't] lie
2 do not[don't] agree
3 do not[don't] enjoy
4 does not[doesn't] have

C
1 Does, talk, doesn't 2 Do, like, do
3 Does, wait, does

D
1 Do you believe 2 Does Henry have
3 His father does not[doesn't] eat
4 I do not[don't] use

UNIT 03 일반동사의 과거형

p.18

A
1 did 2 enjoyed 3 woke
4 dropped 5 worried

B
1 saved 2 married 3 wrote
4 had

C
1 My sister helped me last week
2 We planned the party last Sunday
3 He told a secret to us yesterday
4 She drank much coffee three hours ago

D
1 John called 2 Betty cried
3 The woman bought 4 They sat

UNIT 04 일반동사 과거형의 부정문과 의문문

p.19

A
1 arrive 2 Did 3 buy
4 didn't

B
1 did not[didn't] shop
2 did not[didn't] water
3 did not[didn't] understand
4 did not[didn't] finish

C
1 Did Sam send, didn't
2 Did the boys join, didn't
3 Did you go, did

D
1 Did Judy borrow
2 Did the bakery close
3 His son did not[didn't] read
4 Olivia and I did not[didn't] get

Writing Exercise +

p.20

A
1 found 2 swam 3 doesn't
4 need 5 Did 6 uploaded
7 carries

B
1 It didn't snow a lot last winter
2 Do they change clothes after school
3 We don't watch a baseball game on Mondays
4 Did Simon come from Singapore
5 My sister didn't meet her best friend last Saturday
6 Does he call his grandparents every morning

C
1 Chris told the story
2 We did not touch the painting
3 Do you learn history
4 He does not write in his diary
5 Did Rachel miss the flight
6 My dad washes his car

D
1 Does he like spicy food
2 We heard her voice
3 Did you see Mr. Wood
4 Does Mary cook dinner
5 My friends do not[don't] say bad words
6 She did not[didn't] give the key

Chapter 05 형용사와 부사

UNIT 01 형용사

p.22

A 1 red nose 2 healthy 3 any

B 1 They got some information
2 Laura wanted something different
3 There is a beautiful garden

C 1 any fish 2 some birds
3 many cities 4 much sugar

D 1 anything wrong 2 short story
3 something interesting

UNIT 02 부사

p.23

A 1 ⓑ 2 ⓒ 3 ⓓ
4 ⓐ

B 1 high 2 happily 3 Luckily
4 is always 5 late

C 1 Eddie is sometimes shy
2 It often rains a lot in Korea
3 They are never quiet in class
4 I usually clean my room on the weekend

D 1 safely 2 quietly 3 hard
4 always read

Writing Exercise ✚

p.24

A 1 any 2 lovely 3 O
4 high 5 well 6 O
7 anything strange 8 wisely

B 1 ① slowly ② slow
2 ① gentle ② gently
3 ① carefully ② careful
4 ① surprising ② Surprisingly
5 ① fast ② fast
6 ① early ② early

C 1 warm 2 really 3 seldom takes
4 many deer 5 late
6 any musical instruments

D 1 was very amazing
2 doesn't have much money
3 sells popular desserts
4 usually wears glasses
5 gave some orange juice
6 planned something fun

Chapter 06 현재진행시제와 미래시제

UNIT 01 현재진행시제

p.26

A 1 brushing 2 am not talking
3 putting 4 Sally using
5 tying

B 1 Are they eating
2 Mr. Olson is not[isn't] parking
3 I am not[I'm not] looking
4 Is my sister choosing

C 1 Is, taking 2 Are, drawing
3 Is, swimming

D 1 Robert is not[isn't] lying
2 She is[She's] baking
3 Are you sending

UNIT 02 미래시제

p.27

A 1 won't 2 aren't going 3 prepare
4 Are

B 1 will practice
2 Are, going to buy
3 will not[won't] change

C 1 Will she like
2 He is[He's] going to be busy
3 Are you going to eat
4 Helen won't[will not] exercise

D 1 Is Mandy going to marry
2 Daniel will not[won't] forgive
3 Will they join

Writing Exercise ✛   p.28

A
1 is not[isn't] checking
2 O
3 will not[won't] have
4 will propose
5 going to borrow
6 O
7 bring
8 is not[isn't] going to

B
1 Will she be
2 I will not[won't] forget
3 Are they planning
4 Jenny is not[isn't] listening
5 Is he going to see
6 My friends are not[aren't] going to go

C
1 Is Bob studying
2 Will you download
3 They are[They're] shopping
4 Amanda will not[won't] visit
5 We are[We're] going to graduate

D
1 Will it be windy
2 The babies are not crying
3 Linda is going to cut her hair
4 We will not waste our time
5 My brother is shaking hands
6 Is Jeffrey going to help you
7 I am not going to make the same mistake

Chapter 07 조동사

UNIT 01 can, may

    p.30

A
1 pass   2 may take   3 can't
4 I bring

B
1 ⓑ   2 ⓐ   3 ⓒ
4 ⓑ

C
1 may know   2 cannot[can't] buy
3 may invite   4 can arrive

D
1 Can[May] I change
2 My brother cannot[can't] lift
3 Ms. Green may be

UNIT 02 must, have to

    p.31

A
1 eat   2 doesn't
3 have   4 not throw

B
1 must not   2 don't have to
3 must not   4 doesn't have to

C
1 must clean   2 doesn't have to cook
3 has to visit   4 must not eat

D
1 We must not swim
2 Janet has to change
3 Students must turn off
4 You don't have to buy

Writing Exercise ✛   p.32

A
1 may come   2 has to
3 teach   4 O
5 O   6 must not
7 O   8 doesn't have to

B
1 has to wear   2 Can, understand
3 must not leave   4 cannot[can't] go
5 may be

C
1 must take
2 can[may] watch
3 Can, play
4 don't have to climb
5 cannot[can't] finish
6 have to use

D
1 Can I plant flowers
2 They must not enter this building
3 She may know my name
4 May I join the science club
5 You can borrow my laptop
6 Tom doesn't have to send an e-mail

Chapter 08 동사의 종류

UNIT 01 감각동사

p.34

A 1 nice 2 feels 3 healthy
4 sounds like 5 amazing

B 1 sounded 2 looked like 3 felt
4 tasted

C 1 This puzzle looks difficult
2 The perfume smells good
3 The cookie tastes like blueberries
4 Her answer sounded perfect

D 1 tastes salty 2 felt thirsty
3 smells like roses 4 looks safe

UNIT 02 수여동사

p.35

A 1 us art 2 for 3 us

B 1 sent 2 made 3 passed
4 told

C 1 lent some money to her brother
2 got the new student a chair
3 will find the book for me

D 1 cooked us pizza
2 asked some questions of her father
3 gave me a watch
4 will read newspapers to sick people

Writing Exercise ✚

p.36

A 1 for 2 lovely 3 smells like
4 O 5 happy
6 a bicycle to me[me a bicycle]
7 O 8 to

B 1 felt 2 tasted 3 sounded like
4 wrote 5 got 6 cooked

C 1 smells bad
2 taste like butter
3 made sandwiches for them
4 feels lonely
5 sent old pictures to me
6 showed his friend a new smartphone

D 1 Your aunt looks young
2 Jerry passed Megan the spoon
3 They brought small gifts to the visitors
4 The news sounded like a lie
5 Ms. Lee teaches Korean to foreigners
6 The reporters asked the singer many questions

Chapter 09 전치사

UNIT 01 장소를 나타내는 전치사

p.38

A 1 at 2 under 3 on
4 them

B 1 on 2 at 3 next to
4 in

C 1 in front of me
2 in the bag
3 behind the guide

D 1 Tina at the bus stop
2 music next to him
3 water on her pants

UNIT 02 시간을 나타내는 전치사

p.39

A 1 in 2 after 3 at
4 for

B 1 during 2 for 3 for
4 during

C 1 before 2 in 3 during
4 on

D 1 on her birthday
2 before 4 o'clock
3 after dinner
4 for three months

Writing Exercise ✚
p.40

A
1 at   2 in   3 on
4 O   5 at   6 O

B
1 in   2 under   3 for
4 before   5 at

C
1 for two hours   2 on the paper
3 before lunch   4 under the bridge
5 after school
6 in front of the art museum

D
1 is next to Spain
2 eat songpyeon on Chuseok
3 parked behind the building
4 collected magnets during the trip
5 are sitting on the bench
6 invented the telephone in 1876

Chapter 10 접속사

UNIT 01 and, but, or
p.42

A
1 and   2 or   3 and
4 but

B
1 ① and   ② or
2 ① or   ② but
3 ① but   ② and

C
1 but   2 and   3 or

D
1 in March or in April
2 short but good at sports
3 prepares dinner and washes the dishes

UNIT 02 when, before, after, because
p.43

A
1 before   2 because   3 saves
4 when

B
1 after you made a mistake
2 because he had an accident
3 before we cross the street

C
1 after his team lost
2 when we exercise
3 because my puppy hurt
4 before it gets

D
1 because I am[I'm] busy
2 when the sun shines
3 After he washes the tomatoes

Writing Exercise ✚
p.44

A
1 because I can go skiing
2 and a coat
3 When you need my help
4 or take the subway
5 but he didn't read them
6 after it became popular

B
1 when   2 but   3 or
4 because   5 and   6 before

C
1 before the store opened
2 but my mother found it
3 After Miranda listened to his song
4 and played computer games
5 because the babies are sleeping
6 when she was young

D
1 water and sunlight
2 because he stayed up late
3 after the rain stops
4 when you swim in the ocean
5 before the class started
6 an e-mail or a text message

Chapter 11 문장의 종류

UNIT 01 의문사 의문문 I
p.46

A
1 Who   2 What   3 Whom
4 Whose   5 What

B
1 Who   2 What   3 Whose
4 What

C
1 Who   2 What   3 Who
4 What

D
1 Who fixed my computer
2 What did you learn
3 Whose phone number is this

UNIT 02 의문사 의문문 II

A   p.47
1 Where   2 How much   3 What time

B
1 When   2 How   3 Where
4 How many

C
1 When   2 How far   3 How often
4 Why

D
1 Why do you exercise
2 How long do turtles live
3 How did she hear the rumor

D
1 Let's plant trees
2 Don't push that button
3 When did you buy the laptop
4 What an easy question it is
5 Where did the accident happen
6 How many floors does the tower have

UNIT 03 명령문, 청유문, 감탄문

A   p.48
1 Speak   2 it is   3 How
4 not   5 Be

B
1 Let's eat   2 Don't worry
3 Let's not play   4 Stand up

C
1 How big   2 What great pictures
3 How heavily

D
1 Don't[Do not] run   2 How clever
3 Let's make   4 What surprising news

Writing Exercise +
p.49

A
1 Who   2 When   3 How much
4 Why   5 How old   6 Where
7 Whose

B
1 What a famous actor (he is)
2 Don't[Do not] be shy
3 Bring the sketchbook
4 How quietly she walks
5 Don't[Do not] touch the screen
6 Lock the door
7 How cheap (those apples are)
8 Don't[Do not] paint on the wall

C
1 Turn off
2 Why do you learn
3 How interesting
4 What is the date
5 Let's not tell
6 Who(m) did Linda see

MEMO

MEMO